TECHNICAL REPORT

Gender Differences in Major Federal External Grant Programs

Susan D. Hosek, Amy G. Cox, Bonnie Ghosh-Dastidar,
Aaron Kofner, Nishal Ramphal, Jon Scott,
Sandra H. Berry

Sponsored by the National Science Foundation

RAND INFRASTRUCTURE, SAFETY, AND ENVIRONMENT

This research was sponsored by the National Science Foundation under Contract ENG-9812731 and was conducted within RAND Infrastructure, Safety, and Environment (ISE), a division of the RAND Corporation.

Library of Congress Cataloging-in-Publication Data is available for this publication.

ISBN 0-8330-3854-0

The RAND Corporation is a nonprofit research organization providing objective analysis and effective solutions that address the challenges facing the public and private sectors around the world. RAND's publications do not necessarily reflect the opinions of its research clients and sponsors.

RAND® is a registered trademark.

Published 2005 by the RAND Corporation
1776 Main Street, P.O. Box 2138, Santa Monica, CA 90407-2138
1200 South Hayes Street, Arlington, VA 22202-5050
201 North Craig Street, Suite 202, Pittsburgh, PA 15213-1516
RAND URL: http://www.rand.org/
To order RAND documents or to obtain additional information, contact
Distribution Services: Telephone: (310) 451-7002;
Fax: (310) 451-6915; Email: order@rand.org

Preface

This report documents a study of gender differences in federal research grant funding. The study satisfies a requirement in the National Science Foundation (NSF) Authorization Act of 2002 (Public Law No. 107-368) to "examine differences in amounts requested and awarded, by gender, in major Federal external grant programs." This was one of two studies NSF was directed to sponsor; the other study, which is assessing the careers of science and engineering faculty, is being conducted by the National Academy of Sciences. This study was conducted by the RAND Science and Technology Policy Institute (S&TPI). With the cessation of RAND's management of S&TPI in November 2003, publication of this work is now occurring under the auspices of RAND Infrastructure, Safety, and Environment (ISE).

This study analyzed data from three federal agencies: NSF, the National Institutes of Health, and the Department of Agriculture. Plans to include data from the Departments of Defense and Energy were dropped because adequate data on grant applications and awards were not available for these two agencies. This analysis of agency data is supplemented by a more limited view of research funding from all federal agencies using data from researcher surveys. This study should be of interest to individuals who work on issues related to the involvement of women in scientific research.

About the Science and Technology Policy Institute

Originally created by Congress in 1991 as the Critical Technologies Institute and renamed in 1998, the Science and Technology Policy Institute is a federally funded research and development center sponsored by the National Science Foundation. S&TPI was managed by the RAND Corporation from 1992 through November 30, 2003.

The Institute's mission has been to help improve public policy by conducting objective, independent research and analysis on policy issues that involve science and technology. To this end, the Institute

- supported the Office of Science and Technology Policy and other Executive Branch agencies, offices, and councils

- helped science and technology decisionmakers understand the likely consequences of their decisions and choose among alternative policies
- helped improve understanding in both the public and private sectors of the ways in which science and technology can better serve national objectives.

In carrying out its mission, the Institute consulted broadly with representatives from private industry, institutions of higher education, and other nonprofit institutions.

RAND Transportation, Space, and Technology Program

This research was conducted under the auspices of the Transportation, Space, and Technology (TST) Program within RAND Infrastructure, Safety, and Environment, a division of the RAND Corporation. The mission of ISE is to improve the development, operation, use, and protection of society's essential man-made and natural assets and to enhance the related social assets of safety and security of individuals in transit and in their workplaces and community. The TST research portfolio encompasses policy areas, including transportation systems, space exploration, information and telecommunications technologies, nano- and biotechnologies, and other aspects of science and technology policy.

Questions or comments about this report should be sent to project leader Susan Hosek (Susan_Hosek@rand.org). Information about the RAND Transportation, Space, and Technology Program is available online (www.rand.org/ise/tech). Inquiries about TST research should be sent to the Program Director (tst@rand.org).

Inquiries regarding RAND Infrastructure, Safety, and Environment may be directed to:

Debra Knopman, Director
1200 South Hayes Street
Arlington, VA 22202-5050
703.413.1100, extension 5667
Email: ise@rand.org
http://www.rand.org/ise

Contents

Figures

Tables

Summary

Introduction

In an amendment to the National Science Foundation (NSF) Authorization Act of 2002, Senator Ron Wyden (D-Ore.) requested that the NSF conduct a study to "assess gender differences in the distribution of external Federal research and development funding." The goal of the Wyden amendment was to determine whether federally funded educational programs other than sports comply with Title IX.

This research addresses this congressional directive. More specifically, the study analyzes administrative data from fiscal years (FYs) 2001 through 2003 describing the outcomes of grant applications submitted by women versus men to federal agencies. The outcomes are the probability of getting funded, the funding requested, the size of the award, and the probability of applying again. The study focuses on three federal agencies: the Department of Health and Human Services (DHHS)—and, in particular, the National Institutes of Health (NIH), which accounts for 99 percent of the research funding in DHHS; the NSF; and the U.S. Department of Agriculture (USDA). In addition, the study provides results of an analysis of the 1999 National Survey of Postsecondary Faculty (NSOPF) and the 2001 Survey of Doctorate Recipients (SDR), which include more-limited information on grant funding provided by all federal agencies.

Key Findings

With two important exceptions, we did not find gender differences in federal grant funding outcomes in this study. At NSF and USDA, over a recent three-year period (2001–2003), there were no differences in the amount of funding requested or awarded. We found the same result when we looked at surveys of scientists, social scientists, and engineers. In one of the surveys (the 1999 NSOPF), there were differences in tabulations of the raw survey results, but those differences disappeared when we adjusted for other characteristics, including the researcher's discipline, institution, experience, and past research output.

The major exception was at NIH, where female applicants in 2001–2003 received on average only 63 percent of the funding that male applicants received. One-third of this gender gap is explained by the underrepresentation of women among top 1 percent award winners. If we eliminate the very large awards and also control for other characteristics — age, academic degree, institution, grant type, institute, and year — the difference narrows again. Nevertheless, the gender gap is still 17 percent, which means that women still receive only 83 percent of what men receive when it comes to grant funding.

However, several important data limitations inspire caution in reaching conclusions based on these NIH results. First, NIH does not retain information about co-investigators in its applicant data system. Thus, these results are for principal investigators only. This is likely to be especially important in measuring gender differences in NIH grants because a number of awards there fund larger research teams on which, in some cases, others will do the bulk of the research. Second, some important covariates are unavailable in the NIH data. Unlike both NSF and USDA, the program type at NIH does not convey information about academic discipline. Unlike the case for NSF, we have no information about the research ranking of the university the applicant is from. Finally, the data set we received from NIH did not include the amount of funding requested. Consequently, we cannot determine whether the gender differences in funding awarded reflect applicant decisions about how to request, agency decisions about how much to award, or both. If these covariates affect the funding NIH awards as they do at NSF, it is quite possible that the gender gap would be smaller if we could control for them.

The second area where we found gender differences was in the fraction of first-year applicants who submit another proposal in the following two years. At NSF and NIH, women who applied in 2001 were less likely to apply again. The difference was much larger at NIH (more than 20 percent) than at NSF (5 percent), and it applied to both successful and unsuccessful applicants in the first year. At USDA, we also saw a similar gender gap among those who were successful in the initial year but not among those who were rejected; however, the difference largely disappeared when we controlled for other characteristics. We hypothesize that subsequent application rates may reflect underlying gender differences in application propensity, similar to what another study found in Britain. However, absent a more direct measure of application behavior, we cannot confirm our hypothesis. If women are in fact less likely to apply for funding, female and male applicants for federal research grants likely differ in ways not observed in the data sets we employed for this study, especially at NIH, where the difference is sizable. If application behavior were collected, methods are available to correct for these unobserved differences and further our understanding of gender differences in grant funding.

Future Directions

Our understanding of gender differences in federal research funding is incomplete. However, those interested in the representation of women in the federally funded research community may want to focus first on the representation of women in the applicant pool and their decisions to apply for grants. Women accounted for 21–28 percent of applicants to NSF, NIH, and USDA in recent years and for 25 percent of the survey subsamples of university and medical school researchers we analyzed. This is similar to women's representation in the population of doctoral recipients working in science and engineering. Our study showed again that female researchers have followed somewhat different career paths than male researchers have. In particular, women are less likely to be employed in the major research universities, where most research grants are awarded.

The companion study to ours, which is being conducted at the National Academy of Sciences, will provide more information on career paths of scientists and engineers but not on grant application behavior. Future research on women in science and engineering should address application.

Finally, we note numerous limitations in the information collected in federal agencies' grant application and award data systems. Such limitations hinder the ability to track gender differences in federal grant funding. Better tracking of gender differences in such funding would require that all agencies awarding significant grant funding do the following:

- Maintain a data system that stores information on all grant applications and investigators, including co-investigators. Ideally, each agency would have a single data system rather than separate systems for each subagency or grant program and the agencies would agree on a common list of key data elements.

- Include in the application form key personal characteristics for each investigator, including gender, race and ethnicity, institution (in a way that can be easily categorized), type of academic appointment for investigators in postsecondary education, discipline, degree, and year of degree.

- Fill in missing personal information, including gender, where possible from other applications by the same investigator.

- Record the amount requested and awarded for each proposal and any score assigned to it by the peer reviewers.

- Clearly identify initial proposals and awards, supplements that involve new funding, and amendments that involve no new funding.

Acknowledgments

We are grateful for the support we received from our John Tsapogas, our project officer in the Division of Science Resource Statistics at NSF, and Lynda Carlson, director of the division. The administrative data sets used in this report were provided by Vernon Ross, Chief of the Budget Operations and Systems Branch at NSF; Dorette Finch, Acting Director of the Office of Reports & Analysis, and Bob Moore, both at NIH; and Mark Poth, Director of Competitive Programs in the Cooperative State Research, Education, and Extension Service at USDA.

We would also like to thank our RAND colleagues who contributed in various ways to the project. Matt Schonlau provided us with the Stata code for generating predicted outcome by gender and bootstrapping the standard errors for the associated gender differences. Jonathan Grant and Julie Zissimopoulos made a number of valuable suggestions in their reviews of an earlier draft. Paul Steinberg drafted the summary and research brief for the report.

Abbreviations

CSREES	Cooperative State Research, Education, and Extension Service
DARPA	Defense Advanced Research Projects Agency
DHHS	Department of Health and Human Services
DoD	Department of Defense
DOE	Department of Energy
FY	Fiscal year
GLM	Generalized linear model
MBRS	Minority-Based Research Support
NAS	National Academy of Sciences
NIH	National Institutes of Health
NRI	National Research Institute
NSF	National Science Foundation
NSOPF	National Survey of Postsecondary Faculty
OEP	Office of Extramural Programs (USDA)
PI	Principal investigator
R&D	Research and development
REEd	Research, Education, and Economics division
RFA	Request for Applications
RPG	Research Project Grant

SDR	Survey of Doctorate Recipients
SSA	(U.S.) Social Security Administration
USDA	U.S. Department of Agriculture

1. Introduction

The National Science Foundation (NSF) Authorization Act of 2002 requested a study to "assess gender differences in the distribution of external Federal research and development funding. This study shall examine differences in amounts requested and awarded, by gender, in major Federal external grant programs." This report documents the research conducted at the request of NSF to satisfy this congressional directive.

The study was added to the authorization bill in an amendment, sponsored by Senator Ron Wyden (D-Ore.), that also asked the National Academy of Sciences (NAS) to assess how universities treat female science and engineering faculty members in hiring, promotion, tenure, and allocation of such resources as lab space. The purpose of the Wyden amendment was to determine whether federally funded educational programs other than sports comply with Title IX, which is broadly construed:

> No person in the United States shall, on the basis of sex, be excluded from participation in, be denied the benefits of, or be subjected to discrimination under any educational program or activity receiving Federal financial assistance.

Recent reports from the National Research Council (Long, 2001) and NSF (NSF, 2004) concluded that, whereas the representation of women among scientists and engineers has increased substantially in recent decades, women continue to be underrepresented in many disciplines and are less likely to be in tenure-track positions in major research universities or obtain tenure and rise to higher ranks.

Especially at research universities, federal grant funding provides the resources for conducting research needed to achieve tenure and promotion in the sciences and engineering. In some cases—e.g., public health, biology—salaries are at least partially conditional on grant funding. This is why the Wyden amendment called for a study of gender differences in federal grant funding to complement additional research on outcomes for women in science and engineering careers.

Our research contributes to a limited literature of gender differences in research funding (summarized in Appendix A). Two previous studies of research grant awards in Britain concluded that women are less likely to apply for grants than men, but among those who do apply, the award rates are similar (Grant and Low, 1997; Blake and La Valle, 2000). We found no similarly general studies of research grant funding outcomes for the United States.

We analyze administrative data describing the outcomes of grant applications submitted to federal agencies, generally from fiscal years (FYs) 2001 through 2003. We also provide the results of some limited analysis of the 1999 National Survey of Postsecondary Faculty (NSOPF) and 2001 Survey of Doctorate Recipients (SDR), which included more limited information on grant funding provided by all federal agencies.

Table 1.1
Federal Basic and Applied Research Budget Authority by Agency
FY 2001

Federal Agency	Basic and Applied Research Budget ($ billions)	Percentage
Included in Study		
DHHS	20.67	48.2
NSF	3.05	7.1
USDA	1.81	4.2
Other Agencies		
Department of Defense	4.98	11.6
Department of Energy	4.71	11.0
National Aeronautics and Space Administration	4.19	9.8
All Others	2.86	6.7
Total	42.87	100.0

SOURCE: RaDiUS, https://radius.rand.org/radius/federal_rd.html.

The federal government provided almost $43 billion for basic and applied research in FY 2001, the first year we studied. Table 1.1 shows, for FY 2001, total budget authority for research activities by each federal agency with more than $1 billion in that year. We planned to analyze data from the first five agencies shown in Table 1.1: the Department of Health and Human Services (DHHS)— specifically the National Institutes of Health (NIH); NSF; and the Departments of Defense (DoD), Agriculture (USDA), and Energy (DOE). Subsequently, we dropped DoD and DOE because of shortcomings in their data. DoD grants are awarded by various agencies in the department, but the largest grant programs belong to the Defense Advanced Research Projects Agency (DARPA) and the Army, Navy, and Air Force research offices and medical departments. The data systems at these DoD organizations are minimal. DARPA's system does not consistently record any investigator information, and the other organizations record only the name and address of the investigator(s). DOE's system includes information on grant awards, but not on grant applications.[1]

DHHS, NSF, and USDA accounted for approximately $26 billion, or just over 60 percent, of the total research funding in 2001. Less complete data from the same source (RaDiUS) show that DHHS, NSF, and USDA accounted for 80 percent of all extramural grants in the same year. Within DHHS, 99 percent of research funding is awarded by NIH.

Research Grant Programs in NSF, NIH, and USDA

The importance of grant making varies widely across the three federal agencies we studied. For USDA, the funding of extramural research and development (R&D) accounts for no more than 1 percent of total spending. In contrast, as agencies whose mission is research, NSF and NIH spend about 68 percent and 72 percent, respectively, on extramural R&D.

The allocation of grant-making authority also varies widely across agencies, apparently reflecting the centrality of grant making to the agency's main activities. At USDA, a single department administers the lion's share of R&D awards and dollars, and within this department decisionmaking is concentrated in a single office. At NSF and NIH, at least a dozen departments award grants. However, within these departments final decisions appear to be relatively concentrated.

All agencies make funding opportunities known to the public through program announcements, requests for application, "dear colleague" letters, or some equivalent form of solicitation. Although unsolicited applications for funding are accepted by all agencies, they are far less common than solicited applications.

---

[1] At NSF direction, the National Aeronautics and Space Administration (NASA) was not included in our original list of target agencies. NASA's basic and applied research program awards grants, cooperative agreements, and contracts depending on the submitting organization and other factors. This approach, which is also employed at DARPA, makes the identification of gender differences more problematic than for more homogeneous grant programs.

Each agency uses a slate of different grant mechanisms. The main types include:

- Standard grant, in which the agency provides a specific level of support for a specified period of time with no intent to provide additional future support without submission of another proposal;

- Continuing grant, in which agency provides a specific level of support for an initial specified period of time, say a year, with an intent to provide additional support of the project for additional periods, provided funds are available and the results achieved warrant further support;

- Formula grants, in which payments are made to state land-grant institutions on a formula basis (used by USDA);

- Fellowships or career awards for specific types of researchers, such as predoctorate, postdoctorate, minority, established scientist, and new scientist; and

- Fellowships for specific types of research, such as interactive research, mentored research, technological R&D, research using shared instrumentation, and feasibility research.

These mechanisms are not mutually exclusive, and each agency uses a distinct portfolio of mechanisms. To varying degrees, the agencies also fund research through cooperative agreements and contracts. Typically, contract programs are distinct from grant programs. However, an official at DARPA indicated that the type of institution receiving the award usually determines the funding mechanism it uses; typically, academic institutions receive grants and nonacademic institutions receive contracts.

All five agencies we initially reviewed employ peer review, but their review processes differ by committee size, the mix of internal or external reviewers, whether all proposals are given full review, and who makes final award decisions. At NSF, all applications are fully reviewed by an internal program officer and three to ten external experts, and a division director makes final decisions upon the recommendation of the program officer. NIH's review committees consist of 18 to 20 external experts, led by an internal officer. Based on abbreviated reviews by all committee members, the bottom half of proposals are eliminated without receiving a full review. Two or three committee members review the remaining proposals in depth. Successful proposals are sent to the appropriate institute where final award decisions are made. At USDA, all applications are fully reviewed by a team of outside experts (led by an internal officer) and the top 30 percent of applications are funded.

Since reviewers must assess the qualifications of the proposed investigators in addition to the proposal itself, the reviews are not blind (as peer reviews for journal publication are). Further, as we mentioned above, some grant programs are targeted at certain groups of researchers or institutions. NSF has had a grant program targeted at women for some years; the current program is called ADVANCE, Increasing the Participation and Advancement of Women in Science and Engineering Careers. The solicitation for 2005-2006 focuses on institutional leadership and outreach to encourage women in science and engineering careers and does not provide grant funding for research. We found no other programs targeted at women, although all the agencies have clear policies to ensure fairness in the review process and to encourage underrepresented groups, including women, to participate in their research programs.

Evaluation criteria are similar in spirit across organizations. In general, proposals are evaluated by whether they advance knowledge within or across fields; their creativity or innovativeness; the soundness of the approach or methods; the qualifications of the investigators; and the adequacy of the institutional research environment. Other criteria are unique to a particular agency. For example, NSF puts special emphasis on whether the research promotes teaching, training, and learning; whether it includes minorities and women; and whether its results will be widely disseminated. USDA also emphasizes contributions to teaching and agricultural extension.

Organization of the Report

Chapter Two describes our analytic approach. It includes a discussion of the decisionmaking framework governing research grant applications and awards, followed by descriptions of the data and empirical methods. Results are presented in Chapter Three, first from our analysis of application data for each of the three federal agencies (NSF, NIH, and USDA) and then from our analysis of survey information on all federal funding sources. Chapter Four concludes with a discussion of the results.

2. Analytic Framework, Data, and Empirical Methods

The congressional study requests information on gender differences in federal research-grant funding amounts requested and awarded. Funding requests and awards result from decisions made by the agencies (and their peer reviewers) and potential applicants. Agencies decide on their research priorities, manage peer review processes, and make final award decisions. Reviewers "score" proposals based on scientific merit, the credentials of the proposed researchers, and guidance from the agencies. Researchers decide whether to apply for federal grant funding and which agency program to direct their proposal to. Most important, they select colleagues to collaborate with and write the proposals. As we describe below, researchers' prior career and research decisions also influence funding outcomes because they determine who applies and the credentials they present through their curriculum vitae. These many decisions shape the funding outcomes in complex ways in which the role of gender is also complex and easily subject to misinterpretation.

This chapter begins with a discussion of these agency and researcher decisions because they may lead to gender differences in grant application and funding. This discussion will provide context for interpreting our empirical results. We then describe our data and empirical methods.

Agency and Researcher Decisions Relevant to Grant Funding

When agencies direct more funding to certain disciplines and topics, they improve the funding odds for the researchers who propose research in high-priority areas. To the extent that women are disproportionately represented in either high-priority or low-priority areas, their grant funding may be higher or lower than funding for men. Alternatively, changes in agency priorities may have little impact on gender differences in award rates, as researchers will adjust their application decisions to changes in priorities.

The agencies also select peer reviewers, establish the review process and criteria, and make the final funding decisions based on review results. The stated goal is to award research funding on the basis of scientific merit and to avoid bias. Nevertheless, reviewers' judgments about merit will reflect their own research orientation and may have unintended effects on the success rates for different groups of applicants—by gender or other characteristics.

Potential applicants decide whether to apply for a grant, based on the value of research funding to their work, the odds of success, and the cost to them of writing the proposal. They choose among relevant research funding programs, federal and nonfederal, targeting their research ideas to programs where they believe their proposals will be competitive. They often team with other researchers with whom they want to work and who enhance their chances of getting a grant. Teaming may also lower the effort needed to prepare the proposal.

Researchers on a nine-month salary get additional pay from their grants for the summer months. Researchers needing expensive equipment and support staff will place a higher value on funding, as will those in "soft-money" positions who must cover part or all of their salaries through writing grants. Some universities and departments allow or even encourage their permanent faculty to "buy out" some of their teaching time with grants. Finally, grants support graduate students and postdoctoral fellows (who are more numerous in some disciplines, such as biology, than in others).

To understand more about the value of the grant funding across academic disciplines and for researchers holding different types of positions, we conducted a limited number of interviews of university vice presidents, deans, and department chairs. The information from the interviews is summarized in Appendix E. All but one of our informants told us that research funding had become increasingly important at their institution and that the competition is becoming more difficult. Most indicated that getting an award was a factor in tenure decisions. The size of the award was not always considered important, however. The interviews uncovered little organized effort to assist faculty in grant writing or systematically tracking applications and awards.

The odds of success depend primarily on how the peer reviewers "score" the proposal, although the grant program directors have some discretion in final award decisions and they make the final funding decision based on their budgets. Peer reviewers judge both the proposal and the curriculum vitae of the investigators associated with the proposal. Therefore, award decisions reflect the researchers' past accomplishments (which depend on past grant funding) as well as the quality of the proposal. In disciplines where funding is essential for conducting research, researcher careers are built through cycles of proposal writing and research, where success in each activity enhances success in the other activity. New researchers can compete for small grants on the basis of their dissertation research, and they are often included in grant proposals led by more senior researchers, but they need to publish their early research before they can compete for larger grants. Those who navigate this cycle successfully will experience an increase in the odds of success, whereas those who are initially less successful may find it increasingly difficult to compete for funding. If, as seems likely, the latter are more likely than the former to leave positions where grant funding is highly valuable, more experienced researchers may appear to have higher success rates than inexperienced researchers. Applicants from high-ranking research universities are also likely to compete well for grant funding because these positions are filled based on prior research accomplishment and therefore reflect the same factors considered in review. It may also be the case that peer reviewers use institutional research prestige as a signal of quality. If so, the relationship between success and institutional prestige is more direct.

The major cost of proposal writing is the opportunity cost, or value to the researcher of the time needed if it were allocated to other activities instead. The other activities include conducting research, teaching, and personal time. Our data show that individuals in positions that emphasize teaching over research — e.g., liberal arts colleges — write relatively few grant proposals. Major research universities often provide their assistant professor hires with guaranteed summer funding and start-up funding, allowing junior faculty to focus on research and publication in their first few years. Non–tenure track faculty, on the other hand, may need to focus on grant writing early to ensure they can satisfy the requirement to fund themselves after a few years.

As this discussion makes clear, many factors influence decisions to apply for grants and about how much effort to invest in writing proposals. As we discuss in the next section, to a varying extent some of these factors are captured in the agencies' applicant and award data systems. However, other factors are unobserved. To the extent that women and men differ in these unobserved factors or respond to the factors differently, we would measure differences in the application rate for women and the rate for men. Women applicants would be selected differently from men applicants for reasons that we cannot detect in the data. Most important for this study, it is very possible that there would be systematic differences between women and men in unobserved factors that affect award decisions. In this case, we would attribute the effects of these unobserved factors to gender. Unfortunately, data on grant application behavior are generally unavailable. We are able to look at reapplication behavior during the three years captured in our data to see whether there may be gender differences in the propensity to apply for grants that may result in differential selection of women and men into the applicant pool.

We know from other research that female doctoral recipients take career paths different from the ones male doctoral recipients take. Women are more likely to hold positions outside academia, in non–tenure track positions, and at liberal arts colleges, for example. Overall, they are underrepresented in major research universities, where almost all federal grant funding goes.

In measuring gender differences, we have controlled for the effects of the factors we observe in the data. We also provide additional information about selection in the applicant pool through two supplementary analyses. First, we compare NSF, NIH, and USDA applicants to the university researcher populations from which most of these applicants come. This is a simple population comparison, capable of showing only large selection effects. Second, we estimate the fraction of women versus men who apply more than once to NSF, NIH, or USDA during our three-year study period. We anticipate that higher reapplication rates reflect a higher propensity to apply for grant funding. We use these supplementary analyses to establish a context for interpreting our findings on gender differences in grant funding.

Although NSF, NIH, and USDA together account for about 80 percent of federal research grant funding, the gender differences we estimate for these three agencies may not be fully representative of the overall picture when other federal and nonfederal research funding sources are also considered. Therefore, we also analyze the more limited data on research funding available from surveys of academic faculty and doctoral recipients.

Data Sources

The main data sources for this study are the applicant data systems for the three agencies. When proposals are submitted, a record is created with basic information about the proposal and the investigators. NSF maintains separate data systems for proposals and investigators, linked by unique investigator identifiers. These identifiers are used on all proposals submitted to the agency over time, allowing for the creation of investigator proposing and funding histories. NIH and USDA also create unique investigator identifiers but record individual and proposal characteristics in a single data system.

We obtained records for all research grant proposals submitted to the three agencies in 2001–2003 for NSF and NIH, and in 2000–2002 for USDA. Table 2.1 shows the number of proposals, number of unique researchers, and variables in these three years for each agency. The NSF data system is the most comprehensive; it includes all the most important variables for the principal investigator (PI) and up to four co-investigators. USDA also records information on PIs and co-investigators, but the information is very limited. In particular, gender is not recorded, but, as we discuss below, we were able to infer gender from first name in almost all instances. Academic degree and a measure of experience are also missing. NIH maintains a reasonably complete set of individual variables, but it keeps this information only for the principal investigator. NIH did not include information on the funding requested in proposals in the data extract it provided for this study.

Table 2.1
Sample Sizes and Variables in NSF, NIH, and USDA Applicant Data Sets

	NIH	NSF	USDA
Number of proposals	132,368	105,284	13,979
Number of investigators	61,147	80,056	8,038
Proposal variables			
Subagency or program	Institute	Directorate	Program
Type of grant	√	√	
Months/years of request		√	√
Funding requested		√	√
Accepted/rejected	√	√	√
Funding awarded	√	√	√
Months/years of award	√	√	√
Investigators included	PI only	PI, co-investigators	PI, co-investigators
Investigator variables			
Gender	√	√	√
Research institution	Type	Name	Name
Type of degree	√	√	
Experience or age	Age	Experience	

The congressional study request asked for an investigation of differences in funding for individual researchers by gender. Consistent with this focus, we created an investigator-level data set for each agency by aggregating the data for each unique investigator in each of the three years. For NIH, this was straightforward because we only had information about the PI for each proposal. If a PI submitted more than one proposal in a year, we first determined whether any award was made and then summed the award amounts if more than one proposal was funded. If proposals were submitted to different subagencies or for different award types, we coded each subagency and award type. For NSF and USDA, we created a record for the PI and each co-investigator on multiple-investigator awards (40 percent for NSF and 26 percent for USDA) and split the amounts requested and awarded equally among the investigators. Then we aggregated proposals for each investigator using the same method that we used for NIH.

More specific data cleaning requirements differed across the agencies. Below we describe how we created a final data set for each agency. Then we provide a brief description of the two other data sets we used — the NSOPF and the SRD.

NSF Applications

NSF provided data for all initial research grant applications and awards for 2001–2003, omitting contracts and cooperative agreements. We created an individual-level data set with a record for each applicant in each year, as we described above. We then deleted 8,269 investigators whose gender or experience was not recorded, leaving 115,537 person-year observations over the three-year period.[2] We have considerably more observations for NSF than we do for NIH because we have up to five investigators in the NSF records and only the PI in the NIH records. We calculated experience based on the year that the applicant received his or her highest degree.

NSF provided the name of the institution for each investigator and we coded the institutions using the 2000 Carnegie Classification. The Carnegie classification categorizes all colleges and universities in the United States that are degree-granting and accredited by an agency recognized by the U.S. Secretary of Education. The 2000 edition classifies institutions based on their degree-granting activities from 1995–1996 through 1997–1998. We further classified research universities using rankings developed by *TheCenter* at the University of Florida (Lombardi, Capaldi, et al., 2003). *TheCenter* ranks research universities with at least $20 million in annual federal research funding according to nine measures: total research, federal research, endowment assets, annual giving, National Academy members, faculty awards, doctorates granted, postdoctoral appointees, and median SAT scores. These rankings thus combine the overall scale of

---

[2] Race and disability were included in the original data set, but we excluded these variables from our analysis because they were missing for 52 percent and 33 percent of observations, respectively. We also excluded ethnicity even though it was missing for only 9 percent of cases because we excluded race. This information is optional on the application form, as is gender.

research activity at the university and measures of quality. We used the rankings to subdivide the doctoral/research universities into four groups, based on the numbers of measures in which they were in the top 25 or in the 26–50 group: tier 1 (top 15), tier 2 (next 35), tier 3 (all other ranked universities), and unranked universities.

NIH Applications

The data set we received from NIH also included only grant applications and awards. It omitted data for R&D contracts and largely omitted institutional and training grants, which are identified by the grant type. From the original data set including 132,368 proposals, we deleted 35,794 observations that were for grant amendments and supplements and 11,761 for small business grants. Most amendments are for time extensions and other changes that do not involve new funding. We had hoped to retain supplements with new funding because these grants target specific researcher groups, such as minorities. However, our review of the data and discussions with data managers at NIH indicated that coding inconsistencies for these grant records made it impossible to identify the records we should retain. Small business grants accounted for 3 percent of the total funding during the three years, excluding amendments and supplements. NIH states that its small business grant programs "seek to increase the participation of small businesses in Federal R&D and to increase private sector commercialization of technology developed through Federal R&D." Thus, these grants have a somewhat different purpose than the other grants in our data file, which are primarily for basic and applied research.

This left us with 84,813 proposals for the 2001–2003 period. We then created an investigator-level data set with a record for each individual who applied in each year. Individuals who apply in more than one year appear more than once in the data set. For those who applied more than once in a year, we aggregated the information for that year as described above. This individual-level data set, which is the basis for all our analyses, has 69,664 person-year observations, of which 3,435 (5 percent) were missing gender.

All but two of the variables are self-evident. To ensure that no individual's identity could be inferred, NIH did not provide us with the name of the institution. However, they did provide the institution type, coded two ways:

- Type of institution based on the Carnegie Classification of Institutions of Higher Education,[3] expanded to identify medical schools and nonacademic institutions (i.e., nonprofit or for-profit research organizations).

- For all types of institutions in the above type), whether or not the PI was at a medical school.

NIH added codes for six additional types of institutions: for-profit organizations, research institutions, foreign institutions, independent hospitals, other higher education institutions, and other domestic institutions. We created a single coding system for institution type, combining the two variables provided by NIH into six categories: medical schools at doctoral/research universities, nonmedical schools at doctoral/research universities, medical schools not affiliated with a doctoral/research university, other research or academic institutions, for-profit institutions, and other institutions

We recoded the numerous NIH award types into five groups, based on their purposes and mean funding levels: large research projects, small research projects, research centers, career awards, and other awards. For a list of the awards types included in each category, see Appendix C.

USDA Applications

The USDA data set also included information on all investigators for each proposal submitted during the three-year period. We created a person-level file using the same methods we used for NSF. This file included 11,213 records, of which 10,550 had complete information.

The original data set was missing gender on 47 percent of the records. Based on first name, we were able to input gender for the vast majority of these missing records. The new data set is missing gender on only 6 percent of the records. Our basic strategy was to compare the first name (or the second name if the first was an initial) of any investigator without a recorded gender to a database of male and female first names. We constructed the database from three sources. The vast majority of the names came from the U.S. Social Security Administration (SSA), which publishes the 100 most frequently used girl and boy names for new babies in the United States, based on social security registration at birth.[4] The

---

[3] Documentation for the 2000 edition, used here, may be found at http://www.carnegiefoundation.org/Classification/.

[4] See http://www.ssa.gov/OACT/babynames/.

SSA publishes this information for the current year and for past decades. We compiled the past ten decades, 1900–1909 through 1990–1999, to create the bulk of our list. We then supplemented this list by having colleagues who speak Hebrew or Hindi identify the gender of remaining unknown names. Finally, we supplemented the database with Russian, Scandinavian, and additional Hindi names from a commercial Web site.[5] The database we constructed totaled 4,959 names — 2,502 female names and 2,457 male names. Of the 6,577 records in the USDA data set that did not have a recorded gender, all but 798 had names that were in our database. A disproportionate number of the remaining 798 reflected Asian descent. We had hoped to code these as well, but were informed that once the name has been translated into English (i.e., without the Chinese/Korean/etc. character), gender cannot be reliably established.[6]

USDA has its own institutional coding system, with 10 categories identifying land-grant universities by year established, other universities and postsecondary institutions, and private organizations. Almost 90 percent of applicants were affiliated with land-grant universities (70 percent) or non–land grant universities and colleges. Therefore, we collapsed the USDA categories into three groups: land-grant universities, other universities, and other institutions. We also added categories for academic department, based on the name of the department. The categories are: biological/medical sciences, other sciences and engineering, social science, plant science, animal science and entomology, water/forest/ environment, and soil/agriculture.

Researcher Surveys

Two federal surveys periodically collect information from researchers on grant funding: the NSOPF and the SDR.[7] The National Center for Educational Statistics has conducted three waves of the NSOPF. The most recent survey available when we started this analysis, fielded in 1999, surveyed a sample of faculty and instructional staff at four-year postsecondary institutions (excluding private not-for-profit institutions). The final NSOPF sample included 17,608 instructional and noninstructional respondents from 960 institutions. We identified 2,619 potential applicants for federal grant funding out of the 17,608

---

[5] http://www.babynology.com/index.html.

[6] The inability to code gender based on Asian first names would pose a larger problem for other agencies that fund research disciplines with a larger fraction of researchers whose ethnicity is Asian.

[7] Documentation on these surveys may be found for NSOPF at http://nces.ed.gov/surveys/nsopf/ and for SDR at http://www.nsf.gov/statistics/showsrvy.cfm ?srvy_CatID=3&srvy_Seri=5.

respondents based on characteristics reported in the survey. The characteristics of the individuals we retained were the following:

- At a medical school, medical center, research university, or other doctoral institutions.

- Principal field of research in one of the disciplines that typically applies to major federal grant programs (e.g., engineering, medicine, science, social science).

- Primary responsibility in fall 1998 was teaching, research, or clinical service, and reported time in research was positive.

- Position was tenure-track faculty, postdoctoral or research fellow/scientist/professor, or principal investigator.

- Highest degree was doctoral degree.

- From the cohorts adequately represented in the agency application data sets: those who received their highest degree in 1961 or later and those born in 1937 or later.

The SDR is a biennial survey of individuals who have received a research doctorate in science, engineering, or health from a U.S. institution and live in the United States. The 2001 survey used here included observations on 31,366 respondents. We identified a subgroup of 9,013 respondents who are potential applicants for federal research grants, using criteria similar to those listed above for the NSOPF.

Empirical Methods

Our primary objective is to estimate gender differences in funding requests and awards. We also estimate gender differences in application propensity because, as we discussed at the beginning of this chapter, selection patterns in application may lead to gender differences in requests and awards. Our main results come from the NSF, NIH, and USDA application data sets, but we obtain further information from the NSOPF and SDR.

Amounts Requested and Awarded for NSF, NIH, and USDA

We want to estimate differences between female and male applicants in:

1. Total amount of funding requested from an agency in a year.

2. Total amount awarded by an agency in a year.

As we discuss below, we estimate the award amount from estimates of its two components:

3. Whether an award is given—i.e., the applicant's proposal(s) is accepted.

4. How much funding is awarded, given that the applicant gets an award.

For each of these four variables, we first provide simple averages for women versus men for each agency over the three years for which we received data (2001–2003).[8] Then we provide adjusted gender differences based on regressions that control for the effects of other factors, such as age or experience, type of research institution the applicant is from, and type of grant program. We explored the data for differential gender effects within each agency—by personal characteristics of the researcher (e.g., experience or age) and across different grant programs or types. Overall, we did not find any evidence to suggest that gender differences were more or less pronounced for different kinds of investigators or grants; the very few exceptions to this are described with the other results.

We use a standard two-part regression model to analyze the amount awarded. The first part estimates the probability that any award is made, and the second part estimates the size of the award conditional on an award being made (i.e., for the population of awardees). We took this approach for two, related reasons. First, it mimics the award decision process, which has two stages: peer review to determine which proposals will likely be funded and agency funding allocation decisions, based on the peer review results. Second, the two-part model fit the data well. Two-thirds to three-quarters of applicants in a year receive no funding, so the large majority of the observations in all three data sets have zero award amounts. A two-stage model takes care of problems that would otherwise arise in data with so many zeros.

Therefore, our analysis of amounts requested and awarded involved a single multiple regression for amount requested and a two-part regression model for whether an award was made and the conditional amount awarded (for awardees only, deleting the zero observations). We used a generalized linear model (GLM) with the gamma distribution for the amounts requested and awarded and a probit model for the dichotomous (yes/no) variable measuring whether an award was made. The generalized linear model avoids specifying a simple linear

---

[8] Tabulations by year show little change during this time period in gender differences.

relationship between the investigator-level variables and the amount awarded, while the gamma distribution can account for large values in the amount awarded.[9]

The NIH award data were especially long-tailed. The average award amount was just over $500,000, but the top 1 percent of awardees received amounts from $7.4 million to $151 million. We attempted to find criteria for identifying outliers, but neither the descriptive statistics on these data nor the award/awardee characteristics provided clear criteria for exclusion. Instead, we arbitrarily deleted the top 1 percent of awardees from the data set used for the GLM regressions and elected to provide only descriptive information on the top 693 awardees.

Based on the regression results, we report estimates of average outcomes for women, average outcomes for men, and average gender differences—all adjusted for the other variables in the regressions. The outcomes are:

- Amount requested

- Amount awarded (unconditional, for all applicants), based on:

  o Probability of getting an award

  o Amount awarded (conditional, for awardees only).

These estimates are based on a prediction technique called recycled prediction (Liao, 1994). This simple method is one way to account for differences in the observed characteristics of the male and female applicants in these data sets. The technique is based on a hypothetical experiment that changes the gender of grant applicants but keeps all their other characteristics unchanged. Using the

---

[9] We investigated several other regression models for the two amount variables: amount requested and amount awarded. Both amounts are distributed with a very long right-side tail. We considered ordinary least squares regression with the logarithmic transformation of the dependent variable and other forms of GLM, including a one-part model (including the zeros), a Poisson, a Negative Binomial, and a Gamma distribution. We considered a smearing approach with the logarithmic transformation method to avoid retransformation bias in the predicted amounts (Duan, 1983). This method grossly overpredicted the amount awarded in the NIH data and for men in the NSF data, even when we used gender-specific smearing factors. Therefore, we resorted to a generalized linear model approach for long-tailed distributions as suggested by Buntin and Zaslavsky (2004) and Manning, Basu, and Mullahy (2003). Under this framework, we fit the entire data (including zeros) and also the conditional distribution (without zeros) with the three standard models—Poisson, Negative Binomial, and Gamma. Further, we specified that the log of the expected value of the distribution is a linear function of the predictors. We assessed the residuals produced by these models for normality, plotted the predicted values against actual values to evaluate the quality of prediction, and conducted a Modified Park test. All of the diagnostics pointed to a two-part regression model with a Gamma distribution for the conditional distribution of award amount given that an award is given.

regression coefficients for the amount requested, for example, we predict the amount that each applicant in the sample would request if the applicant were female and again if the same applicant were male. All other variables are set to the actual values for that applicant in both predictions. We then calculate the difference between the "female" prediction and the "male" prediction for each applicant. Finally, we calculate mean values of the female predictions, male predictions, and gender differences, and we estimate the standard errors for each mean using the bootstrap method (Duan, 1983).

Predictions of the unconditional amount awarded are determined using the same general approach. However, the predicted values for each applicant are determined by multiplying the predicted probabilities of getting an award by the predicted conditional amounts awarded, using the recycled (female and male) predictions for that applicant. We also calculate bootstrapped standard errors for these estimates.

All Federal Grant Awards

For information about all federal grant funding, we used data from the NSOPF and SDR surveys for 1999 and 2001. Information on research funding in the surveys includes:

- NSOPF (for fall 1998): whether a PI or co-investigator for any grants, funding source (federal, state, and local; private; foundation; institution; other), total funding from all sources.

- SDR (in 2000): whether any federal research funding, which agencies provided the funding.

We use these data to estimate gender differences using recycled predictions from a regression analysis, using methods similar to the ones described above. We limit our regression analysis to the two outcome variables available in these data sets: whether the researcher has obtained any federal research funding, and how much funding they have received from federal and other sources. The first outcome variable is of more interest since it is available in both surveys and the information should be relatively easy for respondents to report accurately.

Application Propensity

We could not find any source of information on federal grant applications for a general population of researchers. We provide two kinds of information on application propensity, both of which are limited but together may be useful in deciding how likely gender differences in application are.

First, we analyze the propensity to *reapply* for grants from NSF, NIH, and USDA. For every applicant in the first year of our data, 2000 or 2001, we look ahead to see whether the same person applied again in 2001–2002 or 2002–2003.[10] We used a probit model and recycled gender predictions, as before, to analyze this dichotomous dependent variable.

Second, we calculated rough estimates of the propensity to apply for NSF grants by dividing the population of applicants by an estimate of the population of potential applicants derived from the NSOPF. We limited this exercise to NSF applicants because we could better approximate the applicant pool for NSF than for NIH, where we had information only on PIs, and USDA, whose applicant list is small and hard to isolate in the NSOPF. We estimated the total number of potential applicants, using surveys from the most relevant groups of institutions included in the 1999 NSOPF: 235 research universities and other doctoral institutions. The NSOPF selected all institutions in the United States in fall 1998 into these two categories; 88.5 percent of the research and other doctoral institutions cooperated. Further, the survey proceeded to sample with known probabilities a small portion of all those eligible within the cooperating institutions. We used the sampling and nonresponse weights provided with the survey data to allow us to extrapolate the numbers from the sampled individuals to the population of interest.

---

[10] All three agencies provided a consistent identifier for each applicant, typically an ID that could not be used to determine individual identities.

3. Findings

In this chapter, we present results from our analysis of the three agencies' application data and the two researcher surveys. We begin the agency results with NSF because its data system contains the most information about applicants. For each agency, we first provide basic statistics by gender on funding requests and awards and reapplication rates among applicants in the first year (2001). We follow with a comparison between female and male applicants of the award types they apply for or their individual characteristics that might affect award rates and funding amounts. We conclude with the results of the regression analysis, which adjusts the funding and reapplication data for gender differences in these other characteristics. At the end of the chapter, we turn to the survey data to complement the agency analysis.

Grant Funding Outcomes at NSF, NIH, and USDA

NSF

One-fifth of applicants for NSF grants are women (Table 3.1). Requests for funding average just under $500,000, with women requesting slightly less than men. Averaged across all applicants, including those who receive no award, the gender difference in the amount awarded is more than twice as large as the gender difference in the amount requested. Women are less likely to get an award and, among those who are funded, the award sizes are somewhat smaller for women than for men. Although the large sample size ensures that these gender differences are statistically significant, they are modest in size. A much larger gender difference is seen in the reapplication rate, which was 14 percent higher for male applicants in 2002–2003 than it was for female applicants in the same years.

As we discussed earlier, researchers' competitiveness for grant funding depends on the proposals they submit and the credentials they present in their resumes. None of the agencies capture information about the proposals—e.g., topics, scores from peer review—but they do provide information that likely relates to credentials.

Table 3.1
Funding Requested, Funding Awarded, and Reapplication by Gender,
NSF, 2001–2003

	Women	Men	Percentage Difference
Number of applicants (percentage)	24,860 (21.4%)	47,339 (78.6%)	
Average funding requested	$483,003	$494,228	–2.3%
Average funding awarded	$80,508	$84,970	–5.3%
Percentage getting an award	35.4%	36.6%	–3.3%
Average size of award	$227,720	$232,462	–2.0%
Percentage of 2001 applicants reapplying in 2002–2003	43.9%	51.0%	–13.9%

For example, applicants from major research universities typically have built a stronger portfolio of prior research, especially if they are at a highly ranked university. The same is true for more experienced researchers. We also know which NSF directorate the researcher applied to, which carries information about both disciplinary field and average expected funding rate. Women are more likely than men to apply in the social sciences and education, reflecting their greater numbers in these disciplines (Table 3.2). They are also more likely to be from colleges and nonacademic institutions instead of major research universities and to have master's degrees instead of doctoral degrees. The mean age difference is 4.5 years. These differences may explain the modest gender differences in funding requests and awards that we saw in Table 3.1.

The purpose of our regression analysis is to adjust for these other characteristics to the extent that they are measured in the application data. It is easy to think of characteristics not measured but likely to affect funding outcomes — e.g., publication record, subdiscipline (related to the costs of research), or whether the researcher has a teaching or research-only position (those in research-only positions might need to obtain more funding to cover their salaries). Other characteristics — ability, motivation, and research interests — are inherently difficult to measure and therefore unlikely to be observed in any data source. The adjusted gender differences we present here reflect the effects of the characteristics we can observe, not the characteristics we do not or cannot observe as well as any systematic gender bias arising from differential application decisions.

Table 3.2
Differences in Other Applicant Characteristics by Gender,
NSF, 2001–2003

	Women	Men
Directorate		
Biological sciences	17.8%	14.3%
Computer and information sciences	8.7	12.0
Education and human resources	26.1	13.3
Engineering	10.5	20.0
Geosciences	9.9	19.3
Mathematical and physical sciences	2.1	7.9
Social, behavioral, and economic sciences	18.2	10.0
Director's office	1.1	1.4
Applicant's institute		
Research university — tier 1	10.7	12.0
Research university — tier 2	17.5	20.1
Research university — tier 3	10.9	12.2
Research university — unranked	15.5	17.1
Other university	21.2	19.6
College	11.6	8.6
Nonacademic	12.5	10.4
Applicant's degree		
Doctorate	85.1	93.9
Master's	11.6	4.0
Other	3.3	2.1
Mean experience in years	12.8	17.3

Figures 3.1–3.5 show the funding and reapplication outcomes by gender, controlling for the characteristics listed in Table 3.2 and fiscal year (interacted with directorate except in the reapplication regressions). The estimates are derived from multiple regressions, as described in Chapter Two. The regression coefficients and standard errors may be found in Appendix D.

The effects of the other characteristics are similar across outcome measures. More experienced applicants request more funding and get higher awards; the relationship is quadratic, so that the rate of increase with experience decreases and disappears at about 25 years of experience (or around age 60 for most researchers). Interacting gender and experience, we find evidence that the experience profile is steeper for women than it is for men. The degree and institutional type/ranking variables have the expected effects, because researchers with doctoral degrees and from research universities both request and receive higher funding. They are more likely to receive an award, and the size of their awards is larger. College applicants have outcomes similar to unranked research university applicants. The differences in award size by type of institution are partially explained by differences in the amounts requested. The funding rate and award size varied across program area and fiscal year. Focusing on the two program areas with more female applicants, we find that the funding rate was higher in education and human resources and considerably lower in social, behavioral, and economic sciences. The award size was also lower in the social, behavioral, and economic sciences.

Adjusted gender differences in amounts requested and awarded, averaged over the entire applicant pool, are shown in Figures 3.1 and 3.2. The negative "gender gap" that we saw in the adjusted data in Table 3.1 has disappeared. Women both request and receive slightly more than men, if they have the same characteristics. However, the differences are small and not statistically significant. Controlling for the amount requested slightly increases the mean funding awarded to women, relative to men (as shown by the difference between the right-side and left-side bars in Figure 3.2).

Figure 3.1 — Predicted Mean Funding Requested by Gender, NSF (Controlling for Other Characteristics)

Recall that the estimates for the average amount awarded to women and men are derived from a two-part regression model that estimates first the probability of getting an award and then estimates the size of the award using data for awardees only. The results for the two model components are shown in Figures 3.3 and 3.4. Again, the negative gender difference we saw in the unadjusted data disappears. The small positive differences for women in these adjusted estimates are not statistically significant.

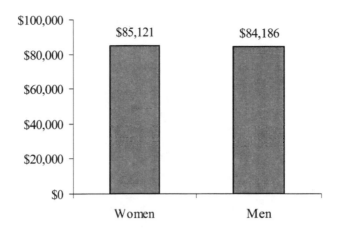

Figure 3.2 — Predicted Mean Funding Awarded by Gender, NSF (Controlling for Other Characteristics)

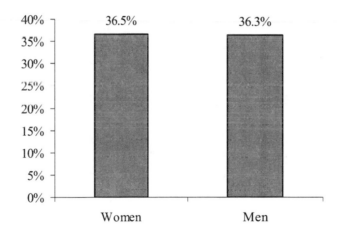

Figure 3.3 — Predicted Probability of Getting an Award by Gender, NSF (Controlling for Other Characteristics)

Summarizing the NSF results, the raw data show a small negative gender gap for women in the amounts requested and awarded. However, the gender gap disappears when we control for gender differences in research discipline, academic degree, experience, and type of institution.[11]

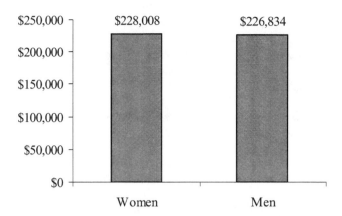

Figure 3.4 — Predicted Award Size (Conditional on Getting an Award), by Gender, NSF (Controlling for Other Characteristics)

Since we observed that women and men differ in the characteristics we observe, it is very possible that they differ in other ways that might affect grant-funding outcomes. As we discussed in Chapter Two, a researcher's propensity to apply for funding depends on a host of factors that may also be expected to affect their funding prospects if they do apply for a grant. Therefore, we can get some indication of whether there are likely to be unobserved gender differences that would change our results from information about application propensity. From the agencies' application data sets we can measure *reapplication* rates, which we take as an indicator of application propensity more generally.

Table 3.3 reports the unadjusted application rates in 2002–2003 for researchers who applied for a grant in 2001. Overall, just under one-half of 2001 applicants applied again in the next two years. Those who received an award in the first year were less likely to apply again and those who were rejected were more likely to apply again. Regardless of the 2001 outcome, women are noticeably less likely to submit another application.

---

[11] NSF makes two types of grant awards: standard awards and continuing awards (see Appendix B). Continuing grants, which tend to be larger, condition funding after the first year on satisfactory progress and budget availability; standard grants do not carry these conditions. We found a modest gender gap for standard grants that is offset by the opposite for continuing grants. With the information available to us, we were not able to explain this difference.

Table 3.3
Percentage of 2001 Applicants Who Apply Again in 2002–2003, by Gender, NSF

	Women	Men	Percentage Difference
All applicants	43.9%	51.0%	–13.9%
Applicants with award in 2001	35.5	41.0	–13.5
Applicants with no award in 2001	47.7	52.2	–13.6

Adjusting for the other characteristics in our data reduces the gender gap in subsequent application in half.[12] The 5 percent difference shown in Figure 3.5 is statistically significant and, as in the raw data, it is unaffected by whether an award was granted in the first year.

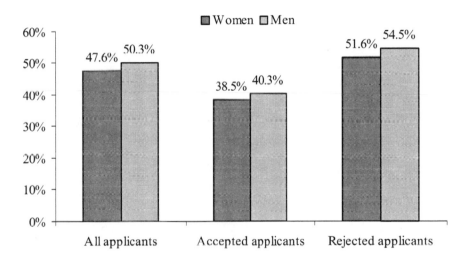

Figure 3.5 — Predicted Probability of Subsequent Application, NSF
(Controlling for Other Characteristics)

NSF is the only agency for which we attempted a rough analysis to assess the application rate for those in the likely applicant pool. As we described in Chapter Two, we calculated the ratio of NSF applicants (unique individuals applying between 2001 and 2003) and an estimate of the applicant pool derived from the NSOPF—for women and for men. We limited both groups to university researchers, who account for almost 90 percent of NSF applicants. For university

---

[12] We ran separate regressions for all applicants, applicants who received an award, and applicants who were rejected in 2001.

researchers, the ratio of female applicants to female potential applicants was 0.49; for men this ratio was 0.57. The gender difference in these very rough numbers is nevertheless consistent with the reapplication rates shown in Table 3.3.

At NSF, we conclude that there is a small negative gender difference in the amounts requested and awarded that is explained by gender differences in research discipline, academic degree, institution type, and experience. We also find that women appear to have a lower propensity to apply for a grant, possibly indicating that unobserved factors are playing a further role in funding outcomes.

NIH

At NIH, close to 30 percent of PIs applying for a grant in 2001–2003 were women (Table 3.4). This is a higher fraction than in the NSF applicant pool because women are better represented in the medical and biological sciences than in the physical sciences and engineering. We did not receive amount requested or information on co-investigators from NIH. Unadjusted results for NIH show that women average less funding than men, as they did at NSF, but the difference is an order of magnitude larger. Women applicants are 11 percent less likely to get any award and, if they do get an award, the amount is almost 30 percent smaller.

Table 3.4
Funding Requested and Funding Awarded by Gender, NIH, 2001–2003

	Women	Men	Percentage Difference
Number of applicants (percent)	18,571 (28.2%)	47,339 (71.8%)	
Average funding requested	NA	NA	
All observations			
Average funding received	$367,842	$582,091	−36.8%
Percentage getting an award	28.7%	32.2%	−10.9%
Average award size	$1,281,679	$1,807,736	−29.1%
Excluding observations with award size above $7.39 million			
Average funding received	$315,968	$417,160	−24.3%
Percentage getting an award	26.3%	29.2%	−9.9%
Average award size	$ 1,200,486	$ 1,427,652	−15.9%

As we explained in Chapter Two, the NIH award data are distributed with a very long right tail and to fit a regression we had to remove the top 1 percent of awards. These 672 awards, which all exceeded $7.39 million, averaged $13.5 million. Women received only 13 percent of these grants, and their average award size was 17 percent lower—$11.4 million versus $13.8 million for men. The bottom three rows in Table 3.4 show the funding outcomes for women and men if we remove these large awards. The underrepresentation of women in the largest grant awards made by NIH accounts for one-third of the gender difference in funding received overall.

Table 3.5 compares the other characteristics of female and male PI applicants at NIH. Women are more likely to apply for small research grants and less likely to apply for large research grants, perhaps because they are somewhat younger. They are less likely to be at a medical school and therefore less likely to have an MD; this may imply that fewer women are in what are usually termed "soft-money" positions requiring significant ongoing grant support. Not shown are the institutes to which applications are submitted, which show modest gender differences with no obvious pattern.

Table 3.5
PI Applicant Characteristics by Gender, NIH

	Women	Men
Award type		
Large research	56.0%	63.0%
Small research	27.2	21.8
Center	2.7	4.7
Career	8.9	5.4
Other	5.3	5.2
Applicant's institute		
Medical school—research university	25.2	30.0
Other medical school	18.3	20.6
Research university—not medical school	30.4	24.5
Other academic	20.0	18.9
Other	0.8	1.1
Applicant's degree		
Ph.D.	75.0	64.2
MD	16.3	22.5
MD-Ph.D.	7.6	12.9
Other	1.1	0.4
Mean age	46.7	48.8

Our regression analysis of NIH funding outcomes excluded the top 1 percent of awards—i.e., observations with awards exceeding $7.39 million. Explanatory variables included the PI's age, academic degree, and institution type (e.g., medical school affiliated with a research university) and the NIH institute(s) and the grant type(s) applied for. The relationship between the funding outcomes— getting an award and award size—and age was described by a cubic function. Success rates and funding awards increased slowly early in the career, accelerated in midcareer, and leveled off in late career. Interacting gender and age, we found no evidence of a gender difference in the age profile of awards. Compared with applicants with a Ph.D. only, those with an MD or both an MD and Ph.D. were more successful. Similarly, applicants from medical schools generally had better outcomes than applicants from other types of research institutions. Funding rates, but not award sizes, declined over the three years (2001–2003), but there were differences across NIH institutes in this time trend.

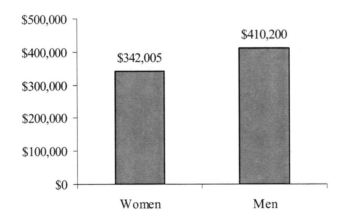

Figure 3.6—Predicted Mean Funding Awarded by Gender, NIH (Controlling for Other Characteristics)

Figures 3.6–3.9 show funding outcomes, predicted from the regression results for women versus men to control for these other, potentially confounding, characteristics. The gender difference in the average amount awarded, shown in Figure 3.6, drops by almost one-third, but it is still 17 percent (compared with the 24 percent difference shown in Table 3.4). Adjusting for other characteristics reduces the gender difference in the probability of getting an award by one-sixth to 8 percent and the difference in award size for those who get an award by two-fifths to 9 percent. Thus, one-half of the 36 percent gender difference in NIH grant-funding awards can be explained by underrepresentation of women PIs in the largest awards and differences in other characteristics associated with gender (e.g., academic degree).[13]

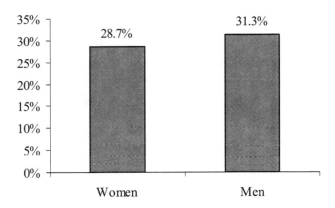

Figure 3.7 — Predicted Probability of Getting an Award by Gender, NIH (Controlling for Other Characteristics)

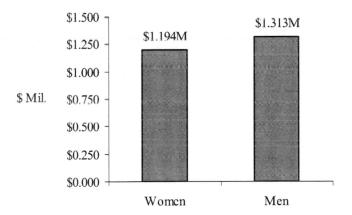

Figure 3.8 — Predicted Award Size, Conditional on Getting an Award, by Gender, NIH (Controlling for Other Characteristics)

The results shown in Figures 3.6–3.8 control for the PI applicant's age, which proxies experience. There is evidence that female researchers acquire less

---

[13] To see whether we might understand better how having data only for PIs might affect our NIH results, we reanalyzed the NSF data focusing only on PIs. The results were virtually the same as what we report above for all investigators. Women represent approximately the same fraction of principal and other investigators in NSF applications. Since the purpose, size, and targeted research areas differ for these two agencies, we hesitate to draw inferences for NIH from this further investigation of the NSF data.

experience with age than male researchers do because they are less likely to be working full time. For example, Long (2001) found that approximately 23 percent of female doctorates in science and engineering were less than fully employed in 1973, compared with only 3 percent of male doctorates. The difference was only half as large in 1995, however. If there were a difference in the rate at which women gain the experience needed to compete successfully for research grants, the effect of age on funding probability and award size would be smaller for women than for men. As we indicated earlier, we did not find this difference when we interacted age and gender. Therefore, it appears unlikely that the gender difference we find in the NIH data is due to the rate at which women versus men gain experience.

As we did for NSF, we look at reapplication rates for women versus men to see whether selection in the applicant pool is likely to affect our estimates of gender differences in funding outcomes. The unadjusted reapplication rates display a large gender difference (Table 3.6). However, in this instance, the difference does not narrow if we control for other characteristics of PI applicants; it remains above 20 percent, suggesting that there may be significant unobserved differences between female and male applicants accounting for the gender difference in funding outcomes that remain after we control for the characteristics we do observe. For example, Table 3.5 shows that women are less likely than men to be at medical schools, suggesting that women may be more likely to send subsequent proposals to other funders instead of NIH.

Table 3.6
Percentage of 2001 Applicants Who Apply Again in 2002–2003, by Gender, NIH

	Women	Men	Percentage Difference
All applicants	14.7%	18.6%	−21.1%
Applicants with award in 2001	23.1	26.8	−14.0
Applicants with no award in 2001	11.4	14.9	−23.3

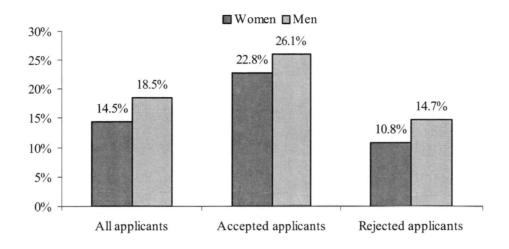

Figure 3.9 — Predicted Probability of Subsequent Application, NIH (Controlling for Other Characteristics)

The gender differences in NIH funding outcomes that we report here should be viewed with caution. Unlike NSF, we lack information on co-investigators, the research ranking of the applicant's institution, and the amount of funding requested by the applicant. We also observe large differences in reapplication rates, suggesting that these or other unobserved characteristics could be behind the gender differences we observe. The limited information we do have explains half of the raw gender differences in the probability of getting an award and the expected award size. More comprehensive data will be necessary to understand why male PIs dominate the largest awards and receive more funding overall.

USDA

In 2001–2003, 23 percent of PI and co-investigator applicants for USDA grants were women (Table 3.7). The average amounts requested were similar for women and men, as were the average funding outcomes.

Table 3.7
Funding Requested and Funding Awarded by Gender,
USDA, 2001–2003

	Women	Men	Percentage Difference
Number of applicants (percentage)	2,452 (23.2%)	8,104 (76.8%)	
Average funding requested	$176,260	$175,285	0.6%
Average funding received	$28,896	$28,222	2.4%
Percentage getting an award	26.1%	25.8%	1.2%
Average award size	$110,542	$109,260	1.2%

Table 3.8
PI/Co-Investigator Applicant Characteristics by Gender, USDA

	Women	Men
Applicant's institution		
Land-grant university	74.4%	79.0%
Other university	20.9	17.0
Other institution	4.8	4.0
Department type		
Biological/medical sciences	24.4	19.8
Other science and engineering	6.6	9.4
Social science	18.9	9.4
Plant science	13.0	13.2
Animal science and entomology	19.0	19.9
Water/forest/environment	10.3	15.2
Soil/agriculture	7.8	13.1

NOTE: Not shown is the percentage of applications submitted to each USDA program and in each year by gender.

Women who apply to USDA are somewhat less likely to be at land-grant universities, where most USDA funding goes, and more likely to be at other types of institutions (see Table 3.8). Consistent with these differences in institution type, female applicants submit more proposals for biomedical or social science research and fewer proposals in traditional agricultural research areas.

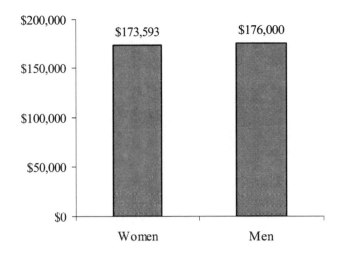

**Figure 3.10 — Predicted Mean Funding Requested by Gender, USDA
(Controlling for Other Characteristics)**

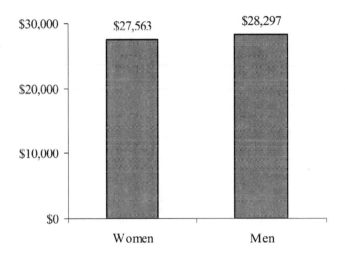

**Figure 3.11 — Predicted Mean Funding Awarded by Gender, USDA
(Controlling for Other Characteristics)**

Figures 3.10 and 3.11 plot estimates of the amounts requested and awarded by gender, controlling for type of research institution and department, fiscal year, and USDA grant program. The differences are small. On average, women request 1.4 percent less than men and receive 2.6 percent less; our estimates show virtually no difference in the probability of getting an award and a small (2.5 percent) difference in award size (see Figures 3.12 and 3.13). However, none of these gender differences is statistically significant. Because the other variables available for USDA applicants are very limited, the adjusted estimates we derive from regression analysis may not be much more indicative of underlying gender differences than the simple statistics in Table 3.7.

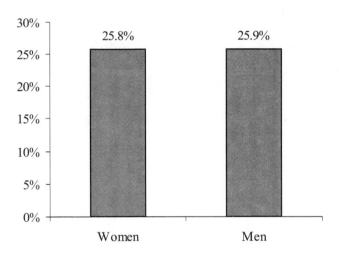

Figure 3.12 — Predicted Probability of Getting an Award by Gender, USDA (Controlling for Other Characteristics)

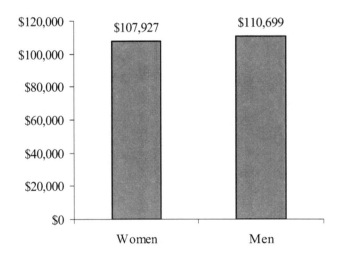

Figure 3.13 — Predicted Award Size by Gender, USDA (Controlling for Other Characteristics)

We turn now to subsequent application rates. Table 3.9 shows very little difference between all 2000 female and male applicants in the fraction submitting proposals again in 2001 or 2002. However, the gender pattern is different for those who were funded in 2000 versus those who were not funded. Among those who were funded in 2000, women were substantially less likely to apply again than men were.

Table 3.9
Percentage of 2000 Applicants Who Apply Again in 2001–2002, by Gender, USDA

	Women	Men	Percentage Difference
All applicants	49.1%	50.0%	–1.8%
Applicants with award in 2000	37.7	45.5	–17.2
Applicants with no award in 2000	53.2	51.7	3.1

The regression results, which control for other characteristics, reflect the pattern that we saw above in the raw data, but the gender differences are smaller and not statistically significant at conventional levels (Figure 3.14). The reapplication rate is lower for women who are funded; however, this difference is statistically significant only at the 0.10 level. Among those not funded, the point estimates show a small positive gender gap that is not statistically significant. Overall, the reapplication rates are almost identical.

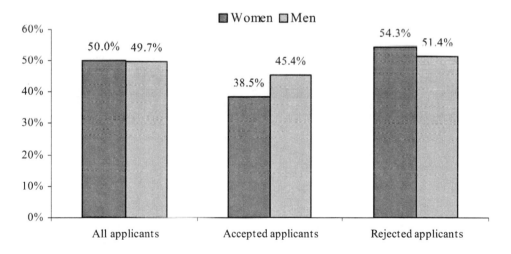

Figure 3.14 – Predicted Probability of Subsequent Application, USDA
(Controlling for Other Characteristics)

Across the board, we find very little gender difference in the USDA grant program — in funding requests, awards, or subsequent application rates. Successful female applicants in 2000 are less likely to apply again in the following two years, but this difference is not statistically significant when we control for other characteristics. It is conceivable that other gender differences might emerge if we had more comprehensive data that would allow us to control for more confounding factors. But based on the information we do have, the experiences of female and male applicants are remarkably similar.

Grant Funding Reported in the Researcher Surveys

To complement our analysis of data from the three federal agencies, we looked at the SDR and NSOPF. As we described in Chapter Two, we selected a subsample of respondents from each survey who were engaged in research at medical schools and universities, which receive the bulk of the federal grant funding for research. The variables available in the public-use versions of these data sets are more extensive for the NSOPF than for the SDR (Table 3.10).

Table 3.10
Variables Available in the NSOPF and SDR Surveys

Variable	NSOPF (1999)	SDR
Federal funding for research	For fall 1998	Yes
Total funding from all sources	For fall 1998	No
Type of academic appointment	Tenured, tenure-track, other	Tenure-track, other
Academic discipline	Physical sciences, social sciences, health sciences, engineering, computer science, agriculture, math/statistics, psychology, education, other	Life sciences, computer/math, physical sciences, social sciences
Type of degree	Ph.D., other doctoral	Not reported
Publications and patents	Peer reviewed, not peer reviewed, books/texts, patents	Not reported
Experience	Yes	Yes

Respondents to both surveys report whether they have federal funding for their research. NSOPF respondents also report their other funding sources and their total funding from all sources. Unfortunately, neither survey asks whether the respondent has applied for funding; this question and a question about total federal funding would be very useful additions for future waves of data collection.

These surveys provide an overview of the role of research funding, from federal and other sources. Overall, 62.5 percent of respondents in the NSOPF subsample of respondents who were engaged in research in fall 1998 indicated that the research had funding support, and 56.5 percent were a PI or co-investigator on at least one grant or contract. Almost three-quarters of those with funding received all or most of it from federal sources. In the SDR, just over one-half of respondents reported receiving federal funding for their research.

Simple tabulations of these survey data yield different results. In the NSOPF, 37 percent of female respondents reported having federal research support—one-quarter less than the 50 percent reported by male respondents. For those with federal support, the mean funding from all sources was also one-quarter lower for women: $202,762 for women versus $269,453 for men. In contrast, there was almost no difference in the fraction of female versus male SDR respondents with funding.

Again using recycled predictions from multiple regressions, we control for the other variables listed in Table 3.10 that might also affect research funding. As Figure 3.15 shows, the other explanatory variables—discipline, degree, institution type, academic appointment, numbers of publications and patents, and experience—explain the gender difference in funding outcomes that we saw in the simple NSOPF tabulations and have essentially no effect on the SDR estimates.[14] In both surveys, we find no gender differences in the fraction of university researchers who have received federal funding when we control for other covariates.

Only the NSOPF survey has any information on the amount of funding received. Figure 3.16 shows the gender differences in funding estimated from a GLM regression. Women report slightly higher funding, but the difference is small (2.4 percent) and not statistically significant.

These results suggest that the gender differences in funding and reapplication remaining after controlling for other characteristics in the NIH data (and, to a

---

[14] In the NSOPF sample, publication/patent history is especially important. If we do not control for the researcher's accomplishments in the NSOPF regressions, we obtain a negative and significant gender difference in whether the person has any research funding. The sample size for estimating differences in funding amount is small.

lesser extent, the NSF data) could be due to other, unobserved differences between women and men.

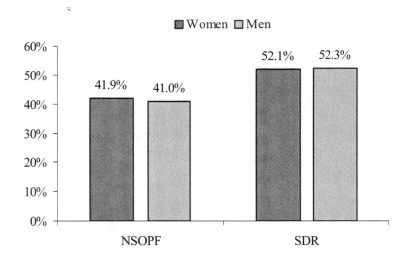

Figure 3.15—Percentage of Researchers at Medical Schools and Universities with
Federal Research Funding by Gender,
1999 NSOPF Versus 2001 SDR

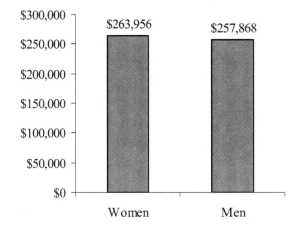

Figure 3.16—Predicted Total Research Funding from All Sources by Gender,
1999 NSOPF

4. Summary and Discussion

With two important exceptions, we did not find gender differences in federal grant funding outcomes in this study. At NSF and USDA, over a recent three-year period, there were no differences in the amount of funding requested or awarded. We found the same result when we looked at surveys of scientists, social scientists, and engineers. In one of the surveys (the 1999 NSOPF), differences cropped up in tabulations of the raw survey results, but there were none when we adjusted for other characteristics including the researcher's discipline, institution, experience, and past research output.

The major exception was at NIH, where female applicants in 2001–2003 received on average only 63 percent of the funding that male applicants received. One-third of this gender gap is explained by the underrepresentation of women among top 1 percent of award winners. If we eliminate the very large awards and also control for other characteristics — age, academic degree, institution, grant type, institute, and year — the difference narrows again. Nevertheless, the gender gap is still 17 percent (women still receive 83 percent of what men receive).

Several important data limitations cause us to be cautious in reaching conclusions based on these NIH results. First, NIH does not retain information about co-investigators in its applicant data system and so these results are for PIs only. This is likely to be an especially important in measuring gender differences in NIH grants because of the number of awards that fund larger research teams, in some of which the bulk of the research will be done by others. Second, some important covariates are unavailable in the NIH data. Unlike both NSF and USDA, the program type at NIH does not convey information about academic discipline. Unlike the case with NSF, we have no information about the research ranking of the university the applicant is from. Finally, the data set we received from NIH did not include the amount of funding requested. Consequently, we cannot determine whether the gender differences in funding awarded reflect applicant decisions about how to request, agency decisions about how much to award, or both. If these covariates affect the funding NIH awards, as they do at NSF, it is quite possible that the gender gap would be smaller if we could control for them.

The second area where we found gender differences was in the fraction of first-year applicants who submit another application in the following two years. At NSF and NIH, women who applied in 2001 were less likely to apply again. The difference was much larger at NIH (more than 20 percent) than at NSF (5 percent), and it applied for both successful and unsuccessful applicants in the first year. At USDA, we also saw a similar gender gap among those who were successful in the initial year, but not among those who were rejected; however, the difference largely disappeared when we controlled for other characteristics. We hypothesize that subsequent application rates may reflect underlying gender differences in application propensity, similar to what a study found in Britain. However, absent a more direct measure of application behavior, we cannot confirm our hypothesis. If women are in fact less likely to apply for funding, female and male applicants for federal research grants likely differ in ways not observed in the data sets we employed for this study, especially at NIH, where the difference is sizable. If application behavior were collected, methods are available to correct for these unobserved differences and further our understanding of gender differences in grant funding.

Our understanding of gender differences in federal research funding is incomplete. However, those interested in the representation of women in the federally funded research community may want to focus first on the representation of women in the applicant pool and their decisions to apply for grants. Women accounted for 21–28 percent of applicants to NSF, NIH, and USDA in recent years and 25 percent of the survey subsamples of university and medical school researchers we analyzed. This is similar to women's representation in the population of doctoral recipients working in science and engineering. Our study showed again that female researchers have followed career paths somewhat different from those of male researchers. In particular, women are less likely to be employed in the major research universities where most research grants are awarded.

The companion study to ours, which is being conducted at NAS, will provide more information on career paths of scientists and engineers but not on grant application behavior. Future research on women in science and engineering should address application.

Finally, we have noted numerous limitations in the information collected in federal agencies' grant application and award data systems. Better tracking of gender differences in federal grant funding would require that all agencies awarding significant grant funding do the following:

- Maintain a data system that stores information on all grant applications and investigators, including co-investigators. Ideally, each agency would have a single data system rather than separate systems for each subagency or grant program, and the agencies would agree on a common list of key data elements.

- Include in the application form key personal characteristics for each investigator, including gender, race and ethnicity, institution (in a way that can be easily categorized), type of academic appointment for investigators in postsecondary education, discipline, degree, and year of degree.

- Fill in missing personal information, including gender, where possible from other applications by the same investigator.

- Record the amount requested and awarded for each proposal and any score assigned to it by the peer reviewers.

- Clearly identify initial proposals and awards, supplements that involve new funding, and amendments that involve no new funding.

Appendix

A. Previous Research

The empirical literature related to gender and the allocation of research funding falls largely into two areas — research related to the actual process of allocating funding and research related to the pool of those applying for funding. Only a few studies directly examine the relationship between gender and research funding. These are complemented by limited research on gender differences in peer-review decisions.

Gender Differences Related to Funding Outcomes

Two recent studies of research funding decisions in Britain and the United States had similar findings: Women were less likely to apply for funding than men, but no gender differences were found in the fraction of applications that were successful. Grant and Low (1997) conducted a comprehensive examination of the largest funder of biomedical research in Great Britain. They looked at grant applications from 1994 to 1996 and found that women applied for grants in far smaller numbers than men did but that, among applicants, award rates were similar for women and men. They also found that, among those who received a grant, publication records were similar for women and men. The same study also found similar results for Britain's Medical Research Council (Grant, Burden, et al., 1997). This research was cited in a decision to require that British Research Councils publish funding outcomes by gender. Similarly, Blake and La Valle (2000) found no evidence of gender discrimination in grant awarding, although women were less likely than men to have applied for grants in the first place. Their findings were based on a survey of researchers at 44 higher educational institutions in Great Britain.

These studies of research funding outcomes in Britain were prompted by Wennerås and Wold (1997), which found striking gender differences in the provision of postdoctoral medical research fellowships in Sweden. Using merged data from the applications and their associated reviews in 1995, they found that women had to be two-and-a-half times as productive as men to receive the same assessment of competence and that women received lower scores on all three areas assessed in a grant application: competency, methodology, and relevance. This research did not assess gender differences in the application rate.

Broder (1993) also found evidence of gender discrimination among male reviewers, but in the opposite direction. For applications for economics research grants to NSF from 1987 to 1990, male reviewers gave women significantly higher scores than they gave men, regardless of the applicant's experience. In contrast, Mastriani and Plattner (1997) concluded that gender had little effect on award decisions in cultural anthropology at NSF.

Because only these few studies examine gender and research funding directly, we also reviewed other research related to the grant award process. We included studies that examine gender differences in manuscript peer review and performance evaluation.

With regard to other aspects of the research funding process, women's and men's funding decisions may be affected indirectly through their relations with other researchers, their institutional prestige, and their topic of study. Gillespie, Chubin, and Kurzon (1985) found that many applicants to NIH are uninformed or misinformed about the grant funding process. Those who are not closely connected to more experienced researchers are thus especially likely to be vulnerable to misinformation. Some studies specifically examine whether academic peer networks may intentionally or unintentionally exclude female researchers and influence funding decisions. Wennerås and Wold (1997) found that being affiliated with one of the reviewers increased applicants' scores in British higher education institutions. Conversely, Travis and Collins (1991) and Cole and Cole (1979) found little evidence of cronyism in British science and engineering funding and in NSF funding, respectively. Note that these studies examined affiliations between applicants and reviewers only and not the potential influence of professional networks on mentoring or grant application writing.

Funding decisions may also be affected by the prestige of the applicant's institution. Cole and Cole (1979) found that prestige had a small to moderate impact on the funding of NSF grant applications. However, a more recent study by Sigelman and Scioli (1987) found no effect of institutional prestige, at least among NSF grants in political science.

What is deemed legitimate research worthy of funding may also be correlated with gender. For example, Grant and Ward (1991) surveyed ten sociology journals over a ten-year period and found that articles about gender-related topics were significantly less likely to note that the authors had external funding than articles on other topics. If this difference reflects funding priorities and women are more likely than men to submit proposals related to gender—two major and unsubstantiated hypotheses—then women could be disadvantaged in funding decisions. Watkins (1993); Rong, Grant, and Ward (1989); and Unger (1983) also find evidence of gender biases in what is considered important topics or methods of study. Because no recent studies exist in this area of research, we do not know whether such biases exist in grant reviews today.

The process of selecting manuscripts for journal publication provides another venue of academic peer review, and several studies have examined whether it has a gender bias. Studies found no evidence of a gender bias in *The American Economic Review* (Blank, 1991) or *The Academy of Management Journal* (Beyer, Chanove, and Fox, 1995).

Gender Differences in the Applicant Pool

The pool of applicants for research funding differs across disciplines and years. Historically, women have been underrepresented in science, and the degree of underrepresentation varies greatly over the last two to three decades and across disciplines. Because the characteristics of the applicant pool contribute to who is likely to apply for research funding and who is likely to receive it, here we briefly review available information on the number of women and men who might be applying for research grants.

NSF recently issued a report on gender differences in the careers of academic scientists and engineers, based on an analysis of the biannual SDR for the years 1981 through 1997 (NSF, 2003). The report concludes that women are less successful than men, as measured by holding a tenure-track position, obtaining tenure, and advancing to higher academic rank. However, the gender differences become statistically insignificant when differences in the influence of marital and parental status are controlled for in the analysis. Characteristics of academic employers and primary work activity did not influence career outcomes during this time period.

Another NSF report (2004) reviewed the literature on gender differences in careers, concluding that the evidence suggests women earn less, are promoted less often, and publish less often than men. Controlling for other factors—e.g., experience, academic rank, publication history, and marital and parental status—narrows the differences but does not eliminate them.

From a survey of faculty, Benjamin (1999) notes that 34 percent of all higher education faculty members were women in the 1997–1998 academic year.

However, not all faculty members are equally likely to apply for federal research funding. Narrowing the potential pool down to those in doctoral degree-granting institutions, which have the greatest emphasis on research, Benjamin (1999) found that fewer faculty members were women — 28 percent. From a 1995 faculty survey, a National Research Council panel concluded that women accounted for 22 percent of faculty in doctoral degree–granting institutions (Long, 2001). In both estimates, the percentages differ greatly by academic rank. Benjamin found that 43 percent of assistant professors, 30 percent of associate professors, and 14 percent of full professors were women.

These differences by professorial rank, combined with dramatic increases in the representation of women in academic faculties since the 1970s (Benjamin, 1999; Long; 2001) suggest that the presence of women in academia is undergoing a cohort-paced change. Long (2001) in particular details the transition over the past several decades among doctoral scientists and engineers. For example, among new Ph.D.s in science (physical, mathematical, life, and social/behavioral sciences and engineering), there were 350 percent more women in 1995 than in 1973.

However, these increases have not been realized evenly across disciplines. In doctoral degree–granting institutions in 1995, women represented 33 percent of faculty in the social and behavioral sciences and 28 percent of faculty in the life sciences but only 11 percent of both mathematical and physical sciences faculty and 6 percent of engineering faculty (Long, 2001). Although change continues to occur — for example, the percentage of new medical school graduates who were women rose from 38 percent to 44 percent between 1992 and 2002 (Barzansky and Etzel, 2003) — the pool of potential research grant applicants clearly has sizable gender differences across disciplines.

Given this variation across academic rank and discipline, we would expect more men to apply for research grants than women in all but some areas of the social sciences. However, the numbers are only part of the story. Applicants' qualifications and constraints affect the likelihood of applying for funding as well. Following the Grant and Low (1997) study, Blake and La Valle (2000) further investigated the rich British data to see why women were less likely than men to apply for research funding in British higher education institutions. They found that both lower qualifications and greater constraints led women to be less likely to apply for funding. On average, women had lower professorial rank, fewer publications, and fewer high-profile activities than their male colleagues. Women also had more family dependents that placed demands on their time, were more likely to have had a break in their employment for family reasons (which related to significantly fewer applications), and reported less institutional support, compared with men. Long (2001) found similar relationships among U.S. women in the sciences. On average, women had less career experience than men in science—up to one year less experience among those who had held their Ph.D.s for 12 years. This is because women have higher rates of part-time work (largely among women with small children), higher rates of unemployment, and slightly higher rates of working outside of science.

In addition to these differences, Long (2001) found differences in graduate training and career paths that likely influenced the preparation of women and men for academic, research-oriented careers. Men were more likely than women to receive graduate funding through research assistantships, which makes them more likely than women to be launched into research careers. In contrast, more women than men funded their graduate work through teaching assistantships in the physical and mathematical sciences and engineering.

Advancing in the professorial ranks requires gaining tenure. Because the tenure decision is typically made when the candidate is in the mid- to late thirties, academic institutions now will extend the tenure clock for maternity and paternity. Thornton (2005) analyzed data from a recent survey of universities and colleges and found that almost 90 percent of Ph.D.-granting institutions had a formal or informal policy to postpone the tenure decision. Relatively few faculty take advantage of these policies, and a gender difference has occurred, with 35 percent of women and 23 percent of men electing to delay tenure. Another notable finding is that 61 percent of the institutions provide no explicit guidance to tenure committees about how to handle tenure delays. The committee members are to use their judgment.

B. Key Features of Major Federal Extramural Research Grant Programs

This appendix provides a description of the grant programs at each of the three agencies we actually studied. The agencies provide detailed information about their programs on their Web sites.

NIH

The major research grant programs are:

- **Research Project Grants** (RPGs) are the most common funding mechanism at NIH. These are generally initiated by the investigator and used to support scientific research or training. A research grant provides a commitment of support for an average of four years of funding. Thus, after the competing year, the grantee receives noncompeting continuations each year for the specified length of the grant. The bulk of funding allocated to RPGs supports noncompeting continuations that allow important research to continue.

- **Research Center Grants** are awarded to extramural research institutions to provide support for long-term multidisciplinary programs of medical research. They also support the development of research resources, aim to integrate basic research with applied research and transfer activities, and promote research in areas of clinical applications with an emphasis on intervention, including prototype development and refinement of products, techniques, processes, methods, and practices.

- **Other Research Grants** consist of a number of activities, including:

  - *Research Career Programs (K awards)* — Designed to provide increased career opportunities in medical research to scientists of superior potential. The program provides support for young investigators who desire advanced development and scientists who need experience to qualify for senior positions. Included within this category are the following awards: Research Career

Development Awards, Clinical Investigator Awards, Academic Investigator Awards, Career Transition Awards, Special Emphasis Research Career Awards, and Physician/Scientist Development Awards.

- o *Cooperative Clinical Research*—Grants awarded to multiple institutions at which investigators are asked to follow common research protocols because insufficient numbers of subjects are available at a single institution to conduct a major clinical trial. NIH staff is substantially involved in the management of these awards.

- o *Minority Biomedical Research Support (MBRS)*—Designed to increase the number and quality of ethnic minority biomedical research scientists by strengthening the capability of eligible institutions to conduct quality research in the health sciences and to support undergraduate students in biomedical research at minority institutions.

NIH consists of 27 institutes and centers (plus the Office of the Director). With one exception, all institutes and centers engage in R&D and all appear to have grant-making authority. The exception is the Center for Scientific Review, which administers the peer-review system.

The National Cancer Institute has the largest budget—18.5 percent of the total budget. It is followed by the National Heart, Lung, and Blood Institute (11.3 percent); the National Institute of Allergy and Infectious Diseases (10.1 percent); the National Institute of General Medical Sciences (7.4 percent); the National Institute of Diabetes and Digestive and Kidney Diseases (6.4 percent); National Institute of Neurological Disorders and Stroke (5.8 percent); and the National Institute of Mental Health (5.5 percent). Together these seven institutes control 65 percent of the total NIH budget and about 90 percent of extramural research spending.

New extramural grant programs and priorities are implemented by publication of one of the following:

- Program Announcement: announces increased priority and/or emphasizes particular funding mechanisms for a specific area of science; applications accepted on standard receipt dates on an ongoing basis.

- Request for Applications (RFA): identifies a more narrowly defined area for which one or more NIH institutes have set aside funds for awarding grants; one receipt date specified in RFA.

- Investigator-Initiated Application: applicant's proposal does not respond to any Program Announcement or RFA but mostly likely relates to the stated program interests of one or more of the institutes or centers. The mechanisms of support for such applications most frequently used are the "R" series of grants, notably the R01 research project grant.[15]

Application and Award Decision

Any individual with the skills, knowledge, and resources necessary to carry out the proposed research may be a principal investigator. In general, individuals from any organization—domestic or foreign, for-profit or nonprofit, public or private, including universities, colleges, hospitals, laboratories, units of state and local governments, eligible agencies of the federal government, and faith-based organizations—may apply. For some specific programs there may be special eligibility requirements, and those requirements are detailed in the Program Announcement or RFA published in the *NIH Guide*. Individuals from underrepresented racial and ethnic groups as well as individuals with disabilities are encouraged to apply. We found no similar statements with regard to women.

Applicants can include a cover letter requesting that their proposal be reviewed by a specific "study section" and/or that the proposal be funded by a particular institute or center.

The Center for Scientific Review receives grant applications, creates a new computer record with a unique identifier for each, assigns applications to an initial review group, and recommends which institutes or centers should fund the proposal. NIH spends six times more on extramural research than on intramural research. The initial review group assigns each proposal to an appropriate "study section" for merit review. Within ten days, the applicant is notified of the study section that will review the proposal and the center or institute that will consider funding it. The applicant may request a change in reviewer or funding center.

_____

[15] http://grants1.nih.gov/grants/funding/giofaq.htm.

Peer Review

A study section is generally composed of 18 to 20 individuals, including a senior administrator. The administrator nominates section members from among active and productive researchers in the biomedical community to serve for multiyear terms. The goal is to have the group's combined knowledge span the diversity of subject matter assigned to the study section for review.

The study section administrator surveys proposals to determine which study section members are best suited to review each proposal (which entails preparing a written report) and/or act as discussants. Typically, two to three members serve as reviewers and two to three serve as discussants.

Six weeks before a study section meeting, all section members are sent all proposals. One week before meeting, each member sends the administrator a list of proposals ranking in the bottom half in terms of scientific merit. A compiled list of bottom-half proposals is prepared. These proposals are not scored or discussed at the meeting; they are returned along with the reviews to the applicant, with opportunity for revision and resubmission.

Meetings usually last two days. Reviewers and discussants present each proposal, after which each section member anonymously assigns each proposal a numerical score. The score reflects the overall impact the project could have on the field based on consideration of the five review criteria (significance, approach, innovation, investigator, and environment), with the emphasis on each criterion varying from one application to another, depending on the nature of the application and its relative strengths. The best possible priority score is 100 and the worst is 500. Within a few days, the scores are entered into a computer that generates an average score and percentile for each proposal. This information is automatically sent to the applicant.

For each proposal discussed at the meeting (about 80), the study section administrator prepares a summary that includes the recommendations of the study section, a recommended budget, and administrative notes of special considerations. The summary and reviews are then sent to the appropriate institute or center. Final award decisions are made at individual institutes and centers; how this is done is less clear.

NSF

NSF awards two types of research grants:

- *Standard Grants* provide a specific level of support for a specified period of time; additional future support requires submission of another proposal.

- *Continuing Grants* fund an initial specified period of time, usually a year, with an intention to continue support of the project for additional specified periods, if the funding is available and the project is proceeding satisfactorily.

R&D grant-making authority resides in nine directorates—Biological Sciences, Computer and Information Science and Engineering, Engineering, Geosciences, Mathematical and Physical Sciences, Social, Behavioral and Economic Sciences, U.S. Polar Research Programs, and U.S. Antarctic Logistical Support Activities. Each directorate houses four to nine more narrowly focused divisions.

Funding opportunities at NSF are announced by use of program announcements, solicitations, and dear colleague letters. The overwhelming majority of proposals are solicited, although unsolicited proposals are also funded.

Application and Award Decision

Proposals received by the NSF Proposal Processing Unit are assigned to the appropriate program for acknowledgement and, if they meet NSF requirements, for peer review.

NSF program officers make award recommendations to their division director, who normally makes final award decisions. Funded proposals go to the Division of Grants and Agreements for review of business, financial, and policy implications and the processing and issuance of a grant or cooperative agreement.

Declined proposals may be resubmitted, but only after substantial revision. Revised proposals are treated as new proposals, subject to the standard review procedures.

Peer Review

A scientist, engineer, or educator serving as an NSF program officer reviews all proposals and submits them to three to ten other researchers outside NSF who are experts in the relevant fields (applicants get nonattributed verbatim copies of peer reviews). Those submitting proposals may include a list of suggested reviewers who they believe are especially well qualified to review the proposal. Applicants also may designate persons they would prefer not to review the proposal, indicating why. The program officer handling the proposal considers the suggestions and may contact the applicant for further information. However, the decision of whether to use the suggestions remains with the program officer.

The two chief criteria used to evaluate proposals are:

- *Intellectual merit:* How does the proposed activity advance knowledge and understanding within its own field or across different fields? How well qualified is the proposer (individual or team) to conduct the project? To what extent does the proposed activity suggest and explore creative and original concepts? How well conceived and organized is the proposed activity? Is there sufficient access to resources?

- *Broader impact:* How well does the activity advance discovery and understanding while promoting teaching, training, and learning? How well does the proposed activity broaden the participation of underrepresented groups (e.g., gender, ethnicity, disability, geographic)? To what extent will it enhance the infrastructure for research and education, such as facilities, instrumentation, networks, and partnerships? Will the results be disseminated broadly to enhance scientific and technological understanding? What may be the benefits of the proposed activity to society?

In addition, NSF gives consideration to two additional criteria:

- *Integration of research and education:* NSF seeks to foster integration of research and education through the programs, projects, and activities it supports at academic and research institutions. At these institutions, individuals may concurrently assume responsibilities as researchers, educators, and students, facilitating connections between research and education.

- *Integrating diversity into NSF programs, projects, and activities:* NSF seeks to broaden opportunities for and enable participation of all citizens—

including women and men, underrepresented minorities, and persons with disabilities — in science and engineering.

USDA

USDA provides two types of grants:

- *Formula Grants:* These grants provide funding to state land-grant universities on a formula basis for a variety of purposes. They are not included in the data for this study.

- *Project Grants*: These are competitive grants, awarded on the basis of peer review.

Intramural and extramural R&D activity appears to originate almost exclusively from the Research, Education, and Economics division (REEd). REEd had four branches: the Agricultural Research Service (ARS), whose function is to conduct intramural research on natural and biological sciences; the Economic Research Service, whose function is to conduct intramural social science and economic research; the National Agricultural Statistics Service, whose main functions are the administer the Census of Agriculture and maintain data on the farm sector; and the Cooperative State Research, Education, and Extension Service (CSREES), part of whose function is to implement extramural R&D programs. CSREES has several funding programs; the National Research Institute (NRI) is the primary competitive research grant program. Beginning in FY 2003, some NRI funding may be directed to projects that integrate research with education and extension activities. Other programs that fund research include Integrated Research, Education, and Extension Competitive Grants to four-year colleges and universities; Sustainable Agriculture Research and Education; the Organic Agriculture Research and Extension Initiative; and Biotechnology Risk Assessment Grants. USDA also has numerous programs that provide institutional grants, especially to land-grant institutions.

CSREES directs its funding to basic and applied projects in 11 areas: agricultural and food biosecurity; agricultural systems; animals and animal products; biotechnology and genomics; economics and commerce; families, youth, and communities; food, nutrition, and health; natural resources and environment; pest management; plants and plant products; and technology and engineering.

Nearly all extramural grant-making authority is centralized in CSREES. Within CSREES, the Office of Extramural Programs (OEP) is responsible for (among other duties) the execution, administration, and payment of formula grants, competitive grants, cooperative agreements, special projects, and other federal-assistance mechanisms.

Application and Award Decision

Ordinarily, applications are submitted in response to an RFA. Application is received by the Proposal Services Unit (presumably part of OEP); checked for completeness, on-time submission, formatting, etc.; and assigned to a grant program, which arranges for peer review.

Sex, race, ethnicity, date of birth, and Social Security number may be voluntarily reported on a form that is attached to the application. This form is detached from application before review. Thus, reviewers presumably do not have access to this information.

The program manager recommends the top 30 percent for funding. Before being sent to the Funds Management Branch, the proposals are reviewed to ensure they comply with OEP legislative rules.

Peer Review

Review committees are composed of three to twelve outside experts from universities and government research facilities. Reviewers for the different research programs use similar criteria to recommend proposals for funding. The NRI criteria are

- scientific merit of the proposed research,

- qualifications of proposed project personnel and adequacy of facilities,

- planning and administration of proposed project, and

- relevance to improvement in and sustainability of U.S. agriculture, including relevance to priority areas or other future issues.

C. Coding of NIH Award Types

Large research grants

R01	Research Project
R18	Research Demonstration and Dissemination Projects
R24	Resource-Related Research Projects
R33	Exploratory/Developmental Grants Phase II
R34	Clinical Trial Planning Grant
R37	Method to Extend Research in Time (MERIT) Award
U01	Research Project (Cooperative Agreements)
U10	Cooperative Clinical Research (Cooperative Agreements)
U18	Research Demonstration (Cooperative Agreements)
U24	Resource-Related Research Project (Cooperative Agreements)
UC1	NIH Challenge Grants and Partnerships Program — Phase II — Cooperative Agreements (NIAID)

Small research grants

R03	Small Research Grants
R15	Academic Research Enhancement Awards (AREA)
R21	Exploratory/Development Grants
R55	James A. Shannon Director's Award

Center grants

G12	Research Centers in Minority Institutions Award
M01	General Clinical Research Centers (NCRR)
P01	Research Program Projects
P20	Exploratory Grants
P30	Center Core Grants
P40	Animal (Mammalian and Nonmammalian) Model, and Animal and Biological Material Resource Grants (NCRR)
P41	Biotechnology Resource Grant Program
P42	Hazardous Substances Basic Research Grants Program (NIEHS)
P50	Specialized Center
P51	Primate Research Center Grants (NCRR)
P60	Comprehensive Center
U19	Research Program (Cooperative Agreement)
U42	Animal (Mammalian and Nonmammalian) Model, and Animal and Biological Materials Resource Cooperative Agreements (NCRR)
U54	Specialized Center (Cooperative Agreements)
U56	Exploratory Grants (Cooperative Agreements) (NCI)

Career grants

K01	Research Scientist Development Award—Research and Training
K02	Research Scientist Development Award—Research
K05	Research Scientist Award
K07	Academic/Teacher Award
K08	Clinical Investigator Award
K12	Physician Scientist Award (Program)
K14	Minority School Faculty Development Award
K18	Career Enhancement Award
K22	Career Transition Award
K23	Mentored Patient-Oriented Research Career Development Award
K24	Midcareer Investigator Award in Patient-Oriented Research
K25	Mentored Quantitative Research Career Development Award
K26	Midcareer Investigator Award in Biomedical and Behavioral Research
K30	Clinical Research Curriculum Award (CRCA)
R29	First Independent Research Support and Transition (FIRST) Award
UH1	Historically Black Colleges and Universities Research Scientist Award

Other

R 13	Conferences
R 25	Education Projects
S 06	Minority Biomedical Research Support—MBRS
S 07	Biomedical Research Support Grants (NCRR)
S 10	Biomedical Research Support Shared Instrumentation Grants (NCRR)
S 11	Minority Biomedical Research Support Thematic Project Grants
S 21	Research and Institutional Resources Health Disparities Endowment Grants—Capacity Building
S 22	Research and Student Resources Health Disparities Endowment Grants—Educational Programs
U 13	Conference (Cooperative Agreement)

D. Regression Results

Table D.1
Recycled Predicted Outcome Variables with Bootstrapped Standard Errors

	Women	Men	Difference	Standard Error
NSF				
$ requested	$500,936	$491,326	$9,610	6390
$ awarded (avg for all applicants)	$85,121	$84,186	$936	1844
% awarded	0.3650	0.3628	0.0022	0.0035
$ awarded (avg for awardees only)	$233,038	$231,837	$1,201	4527
% 2001 applicants who reapply in 2002–2003	0.4763	0.5027	−0.0264	0.0064
Accepted in 2001	0.3845	0.4033	−0.0188	0.0177
Rejected in 2001	0.5164	0.5453	−0.0289	0.0085
NIH				
$ requested	NA	NA	NA	NA
$ awarded (avg for all applicants)	$342,005	$410,200	−$68,195	8,970
% awarded	0.2868	0.3127	−0.0259	0.0047
$ awarded (avg for awardees only)	$1,194,212	$1,313,318	−$119,106	21,052
% 2001 applicants who reapply in 2002–2003	14.48%	18.46%	−3.98%	0.0059
Accepted in 2001	22.79%	26.06%	−3.26%	0.0126
Not accepted in 2001	10.84%	14.74%	−3.91%	0.0063
USDA				
$ requested	$173,593	$176,000	$2,406	3,245
$ awarded (avg for all applicants)	$27,563	$28,297	−$734	1,383
% awarded	0.2584	0.2586	−0.0002	0.0101
$ awarded (avg for awardees only)	$107,927	$110,699	−$2,772	3,702
% 2001 applicants who reapply in 2002–2003	0.5004	0.4967	0.0037	0.0233
Accepted in 2001	0.3854	0.4535	−0.0681	0.0414
Rejected in 2001	0.5432	0.5135	0.0297	0.0202
NSOPF				
% with federal funding	0.4194	0.4101	0.0093	0.0193
$ from all funding sources	$263,956	$257,868	$6,088	25,556
SDR				
% with federal funding	0.5202	0.5227	−0.0024	0.0117

Table D.2
Regression Coefficients and Standard Errors for NSF Funding Requested and Awarded

Variable	$ requested Coef.	$ requested Std. Err.	Whether funded Coef.	Whether funded Std. Err.	$ awarded, if funded Coef.	$ awarded, if funded Std. Err.
Female	0.019370	0.012930	0.005922	0.009705	0.005166	0.018978
Experience	0.032787	0.001621	0.015629	0.001227	0.028429	0.002473
Experience sq	−0.000568	0.000039	−0.000340	0.000030	−0.000449	0.000059
Not_PhD	−0.536650	0.021089	−0.064078	0.015247	−0.376386	0.031830
Research univ, tier 1						
Research univ, tier 2	−0.054742	0.018659	−0.106013	0.013744	−0.130462	0.024873
Research univ, tier 3	−0.137075	0.020816	−0.238927	0.015452	−0.278897	0.028933
Research univ, unranked	−0.261517	0.019290	−0.363400	0.014403	−0.359205	0.027364
Other univ	−0.455936	0.018802	−0.403695	0.014146	−0.546592	0.026827
College	−0.392452	0.022598	−0.188987	0.016869	−0.406021	0.031342
Nonacademic	−0.113634	0.022420	−0.254602	0.016359	0.040001	0.031450
fy2002	−0.113119	0.030170	0.006426	0.022362	0.016153	0.041836
fy2003	−0.162471	0.029567	0.006300	0.021917	0.014462	0.041013
Math & physical sci						
Biological sci	−0.086846	0.031136	−0.189050	0.023335	0.120120	0.045723
Computer sci	0.233466	0.034987	−0.185585	0.026275	0.212051	0.051857
Educ & human res	0.025692	0.032332	0.016167	0.023690	0.238751	0.045249
Other directorates	0.462668	0.074036	−0.044143	0.054903	0.370927	0.105237
Engineering	−0.146407	0.031233	−0.208581	0.023524	−0.169104	0.046502
Geological sci	−0.281008	0.037165	0.255024	0.027332	−0.056267	0.048195
Social, behav sci	−0.673603	0.034280	−0.007723	0.025472	−0.763989	0.047594
yr02_bio	0.156039	0.044108	0.007042	0.033096	−0.013033	0.064682
yr02_comp	0.307470	0.048587	0.013423	0.036508	−0.007712	0.071421
yr02_educ	0.538407	0.043573	−0.191127	0.032530	−0.015231	0.062749
yr02_eng	0.030568	0.043177	0.084546	0.032382	−0.173419	0.063057
yr02_geo	0.238841	0.051356	−0.103428	0.037804	0.095402	0.067342
yr02_social	0.124728	0.047633	−0.081394	0.035376	−0.046816	0.066814
yr02_oth_dir	−0.257085	0.108939	0.333724	0.080296	0.051080	0.144181
yr03_bio	0.317277	0.043169	−0.042139	0.032453	0.079915	0.063796
yr03_comp	0.423490	0.047209	−0.074250	0.035609	−0.000418	0.070355
yr03_educ	0.763960	0.042987	−0.323314	0.032313	0.052773	0.063380
yr03_eng	0.211820	0.041659	−0.004434	0.031343	−0.083956	0.061556
yr03_geo	0.308260	0.050793	−0.097433	0.037397	0.164884	0.066483
yr03_social	0.320907	0.046757	−0.145553	0.034810	0.011282	0.066317
yr03_oth_dir	−0.305223	0.108274	0.320317	0.079844	−0.283726	0.143863
constant	12.985990	0.029101	−0.143754	0.021525	12.289600	0.041118
Observations	115,537		115,537		41,973	
Log likelihood	−1621132.965		−74236.083		−557575.8704	

	All Applicants		Award in 2001		Rejected in 2001	
	Coef.	Std. Err.	Coef.	Std. Err.	Coef.	Std. Err.
Female	−0.069930	0.017615	−0.051361	0.032060	−0.076145	0.021141
Experience	0.001688	0.002192	0.010535	0.004127	−0.001624	0.002603
Experience sq	−0.000237	0.000053	−0.000402	0.000100	−0.000173	0.000064
Not_PhD	−0.571852	0.029015	−0.508748	0.053096	−0.591014	0.034699
Research univ, tier 1						
Research univ, tier 2	0.033979	0.024853	0.067176	0.042170	0.019338	0.030927
Research univ, tier 3	0.005128	0.027502	0.005423	0.048593	0.004071	0.033650
Research univ,						
Unranked univ	−0.037111	0.025774	−0.077214	0.046583	−0.030721	0.031345
Other univ	−0.211097	0.025242	−0.173662	0.045307	−0.230133	0.030751
College	−0.216054	0.030457	−0.252721	0.052689	−0.199782	0.037570
Nonacademic	−0.284834	0.030263	−0.062770	0.053090	−0.384787	0.036975
Math & physical sci						
Biological sci	−0.141786	0.023119	0.019060	0.043790	−0.234090	0.027587
Computer sci	0.113269	0.025832	0.471319	0.050783	−0.040301	0.030347
Educ & human res	−0.135792	0.024585	0.136402	0.043587	−0.274077	0.030045
Other directorates	0.131058	0.053946	0.526493	0.103871	−0.040853	0.063160
Engineering	0.101100	0.023492	0.483006	0.045032	−0.061165	0.027847
Geological sci	0.267546	0.027802	0.551367	0.045256	0.115368	0.035571
Social, behav sci	−0.397431	0.026461	−0.175079	0.046678	−0.512563	0.032343
Constant	0.337364	0.030989	−0.355522	0.054726	0.495103	0.037330
Accepted in 2001	−0.355050	0.015036				
Observations	35,563		10,719		24,844	
Log likelihood	−23385.743		−6869.8963		−16399.072	

Table D.4
Regression Coefficients and Standard Errors for NIH
Funding Awarded

	Whether funded		$ awarded, if funded	
	Coef.	Std. Err.	Coef.	Std. Err.
Female	−0.077712	0.013519	−0.095070	0.017211
Age, mean adj	0.004619	0.001038	0.011107	0.001259
Age squared	0.000197	0.000067	−0.000376	0.000080
Age cubed	−0.000014	0.000004	0.000002	0.000004
PhD				
MD	0.032400	0.027716	0.037894	0.034823
MD/PhD	0.081377	0.037768	0.055561	0.046961
Neither degree	−0.462381	0.104206	−0.756173	0.148876
fy2002	−0.033381	0.013252	0.020997	0.016395
fy2003	−0.103836	0.013340	0.027526	0.016529
Large grants				
Small grants	0.129931	0.013259	−1.181407	0.016637
Center grants	0.333947	0.028366	0.917377	0.031831
Career grants	0.421042	0.021616	−0.652351	0.024772
Other grants	0.852528	0.027363	−0.779855	0.025785
Med sch at univ				
Med sch not at univ	−0.025762	0.015170	−0.036110	0.018691
Nonmed doctoral	−0.112201	0.014865	−0.177230	0.018645
Other acad/res	−0.043264	0.015479	0.019175	0.019124
For profit	−0.736465	0.068444	0.296396	0.111067
Other inst.	−0.142333	0.026366	−0.426709	0.032566
inst1	0.197868	0.037347	0.280196	0.046276
inst2	0.184784	0.025254	0.067096	0.030729
inst3	0.355388	0.019897	0.361606	0.023325
inst4	0.021068	0.029301	0.106277	0.037581
inst5	−0.216931	0.049426	0.318385	0.069367
inst7	0.333848	0.027115	0.334757	0.032027
inst8	0.350896	0.037597	0.199528	0.044930
inst9	0.145746	0.039164	0.258770	0.049206
inst10	0.293462	0.020121	0.197979	0.023586
inst11	0.131762	0.037968	0.527711	0.049538
inst12	0.112511	0.037566	0.288728	0.046655
inst13	0.477215	0.032206	0.276846	0.037049
inst14	0.456492	0.019956	0.222831	0.022946
inst15	0.140978	0.023204	0.254624	0.028831
inst16	0.382588	0.059743	0.268859	0.068857
inst17	0.289080	0.019135	0.289741	0.022449
inst18	0.163056	0.096663	−0.155315	0.120566
inst19	0.479921	0.108405	0.602371	0.110267
inst20	0.017096	0.022630	0.230661	0.028934

	Whether funded		$ awarded, if funded	
	Coef.	Std. Err.	Coef.	Std. Err.
inst21	0.021578	0.054027	−0.151458	0.074121
inst22	0.185088	0.021529	0.248450	0.026185
inst23	0.102954	0.034495	0.208332	0.034402
inst24	0.154625	0.044647	0.274262	0.054688
Constant	−0.743621	0.017544	14.092650	0.020621
Observations	64,824		19,805	
Log likelihood	−38318.078		−294625.2589	

Table D.5
Regression Coefficients and Standard Errors for NIH
Reapplication

	All 2001 applicants		Award in 2001		Rejected in 2001	
	Coef.	Std. Err.	Coef.	Std. Err.	Coef.	Std. Err.
Female	−0.198167	0.031125	−0.131798	0.051693	−0.225660	0.039804
Age, mean adj	0.008205	0.002187	0.002226	0.003663	0.011157	0.002802
Age squared	−0.000650	0.000135	−0.000886	0.000233	−0.000543	0.000169
Age cubed	0.000004	0.000008	0.000030	0.000014	−0.000009	0.000010
PhD						
MD	−0.105200	0.065399	−0.251681	0.104598	−0.042517	0.085464
MD/PhD	0.266513	0.093505	−0.084594	0.149893	0.472884	0.120409
Neither degree	−0.733587	0.252133	−0.753391	0.385109	−0.688504	0.359220
fy2002	0.596824	0.029431	0.630278	0.049121	0.555631	0.037458
fy2003	0.737748	0.059540	0.841000	0.087706	0.567111	0.085204
Large grants						
Small grants	0.023039	0.055225	−0.032735	0.080135	−0.022881	0.078533
Center grants	0.636760	0.057276	0.783707	0.076446	0.125261	0.099139
Career grants	−0.021843	0.032847	−0.057054	0.053301	−0.006670	0.042308
Other grants	−0.273189	0.033706	−0.243866	0.055707	−0.277445	0.043079
Med sch at univ						
Med sch not at univ	−0.061560	0.034098	−0.111686	0.055812	−0.019482	0.043575
Nonmed doctoral	−0.386850	0.158629	0.092090	0.376863	−0.388271	0.178880
Other acad/resarch	−0.433483	0.066977	−0.341634	0.106446	−0.523836	0.091735
inst1	1.132176	0.082042	1.070626	0.141148	1.157680	0.101637
inst2	1.268282	0.052006	1.316778	0.084050	1.208465	0.067390
inst3	1.305314	0.047737	1.327597	0.076272	1.258668	0.062331
inst4	1.252835	0.060663	1.243448	0.099532	1.247289	0.077450
inst5	0.981350	0.090133	0.998814	0.170957	1.014660	0.108121
inst7	1.393563	0.057417	1.417372	0.093321	1.345533	0.073680
inst8	0.866232	0.089419	1.005606	0.133988	0.694552	0.126033
inst9	1.226734	0.089671	1.259061	0.148048	1.212551	0.113716
inst10	1.346806	0.044348	1.404829	0.074505	1.300304	0.056233
inst12	1.290892	0.071822	1.277859	0.118735	1.314660	0.091153
inst13	0.915572	0.079221	0.873204	0.118635	0.883719	0.107716
inst14	1.190807	0.046604	1.140563	0.071612	1.192233	0.062285
inst15	1.131765	0.048977	1.266583	0.081007	1.043451	0.062955
inst16	1.301737	0.151819	1.125299	0.220006	1.446910	0.207614
inst17	1.245183	0.043950	1.310605	0.071159	1.181588	0.056708
inst18	1.105183	0.241818	0.513811	0.477242	1.388396	0.277791
inst19	−0.007559	0.504218			0.294402	0.483750
inst20	1.108991	0.051939	1.177921	0.089649	1.084679	0.064739
inst21	1.032208	0.122196	1.004102	0.217492	1.054145	0.149351
inst22	1.229121	0.048475	1.250886	0.079121	1.194376	0.062258
inst23	0.859027	0.078935	0.723978	0.112485	1.124991	0.116588

	All 2001 applicants		Award in 2001		Rejected in 2001	
	Coef.	Std. Err.	Coef.	Std. Err.	Coef.	Std. Err.
inst24	1.079974	0.117495	0.992731	0.187139	1.110228	0.151885
Constant	−2.193784	0.038250	−2.028037	0.062028	−2.254244	0.049321
Observations	19,565		6,267		13,298	
Log likelihood	−6900.0506		−2679.6467		−4110.9214	

	$ requested		Whether funded		$ awarded, if funded	
	Coef.	Std. Err.	Coef.	Std. Err.	Coef.	Std. Err.
Female	–0.013766	0.018820	–0.000734	0.032251	–0.025359	0.035261
fy2001	–0.023641	0.019575	–0.088751	0.033498	0.004565	0.036398
fy2002	–0.033703	0.020043	0.040536	0.033921	–0.048448	0.036474
Water/forest/env						
Bio/med sciences	–0.048055	0.033266	–0.008236	0.056808	–0.149298	0.063087
Other science/engineering	–0.038019	0.033372	–0.141193	0.057520	0.008915	0.066622
Social sciences	–0.035253	0.030311	0.080846	0.050984	–0.091681	0.055380
Plant science	0.016190	0.027117	0.045728	0.045196	–0.000050	0.049708
Anim science	–0.068922	0.029674	–0.239649	0.052149	–0.179877	0.062883
Soil/agriculture	–0.153128	0.031879	–0.101713	0.054752	–0.268061	0.062837
Non–land grant	0.018770	0.022440	0.014489	0.038660	0.011614	0.042810
Other institution	0.023959	0.040874	0.006391	0.069467	–0.401698	0.076317
prog2	0.341723	0.070559	0.168243	0.120588	0.426072	0.134158
prog3	0.031473	0.063017	0.173165	0.108536	0.062045	0.120532
prog4	0.187921	0.050871	0.212515	0.088909	0.195511	0.100628
prog5	0.220726	0.063611	0.299332	0.108211	0.260862	0.118152
prog6	0.189881	0.056966	0.035887	0.100394	0.182313	0.114902
prog7	0.021855	0.059250	–0.135612	0.106945	0.078111	0.127261
prog8	0.145007	0.061373	0.216875	0.105320	0.118226	0.116883
prog9	–0.154584	0.063361	–0.015437	0.110903	0.011676	0.128280
prog10	0.235877	0.059286	–0.072427	0.104589	0.433321	0.121806
prog11	–0.097177	0.060700	0.074311	0.106151	0.129160	0.121210
prog12	0.347104	0.064192	0.342548	0.108228	0.148788	0.116420
prog13	0.180248	0.072069	0.049447	0.126295	0.111738	0.147028
prog14	0.846747	0.079776	0.055633	0.137838	1.225688	0.156223
prog15	–0.690880	0.072315	1.028361	0.119659	–0.933663	0.114664
prog16	–0.081409	0.055144	–0.137935	0.099337	0.253792	0.117062
prog17	0.411882	0.060767	0.265505	0.103738	0.280091	0.114098
prog18	–0.218750	0.063138	0.248998	0.109529	–0.259871	0.124969
prog19	0.003917	0.055760	0.007933	0.098174	–0.048396	0.114350
prog20	–0.016786	0.055760	0.071745	0.097362	0.149485	0.110980
prog21	0.004882	0.069066	–0.279199	0.128808	0.143922	0.157799
prog22	–0.539659	0.061032	0.390385	0.103833	–0.485165	0.115600
prog23	1.183170	0.090478	–0.851361	0.205269	1.900728	0.304082
prog24	0.330737	0.083218	0.169419	0.140428	0.384553	0.153317
prog25	0.331096	0.060335	0.151921	0.104668	0.194996	0.117792
prog26	–0.354060	0.204703	0.798918	0.323020	–0.293609	0.283338
prog27	1.646843	0.330761			2.177483	0.328329
prog28	–0.432117	0.064314	0.234481	0.111104	–0.503866	0.125589
prog29	–0.804749	0.068019	0.505437	0.113938	–0.608170	0.120056

	$ requested		Whether funded		$ awarded, if funded	
	Coef.	Std. Err.	Coef.	Std. Err.	Coef.	Std. Err.
prog30	0.095778	0.054728	0.046068	0.096887	0.242034	0.113146
prog31	−0.049724	0.052997	−0.150267	0.096554	0.158897	0.116198
Constant	12.032380	0.047253	−0.715724	0.082876	11.568260	0.095956
Observations	10,550		10,550		2,734	
Log likelihood	−137486.4625		−5846.9945		−34253.03894	

Table D.7
Regression Coefficients and Standard Errors for USDA
Reapplication

	All 2000 applicants		Award in 2000		Rejected in 2000	
	Coef.	Std. Err.	Coef.	Std. Err.	Coef.	Std. Err.
Female	0.009630	0.052484	−0.190788	0.105639	0.078935	0.061664
Water/forest/env						
Bio/med sciences	0.210731	0.092107	−0.344713	0.200579	0.385136	0.107825
Other						
science/engineering	0.333743	0.093532	0.357367	0.193435	0.319278	0.108534
Social sciences	0.411544	0.082839	0.293875	0.164780	0.408506	0.097555
Plant science	0.302333	0.071053	0.421534	0.142675	0.273219	0.083855
Anim science	0.346281	0.078121	0.506301	0.171001	0.283920	0.089247
Soil/agriculture	0.281322	0.086781	0.422884	0.173194	0.222579	0.102088
Non–land grant	−0.271530	0.060446	−0.261764	0.128272	−0.333731	0.070204
Other institution	−0.528332	0.117892	−0.197831	0.217050	−0.674063	0.145205
prog2	0.619551	0.188830	0.211151	0.408846	0.763886	0.217406
prog3	0.555367	0.164890	0.276576	0.344481	0.707414	0.192934
prog4	0.645288	0.127246	0.743251	0.284295	0.620070	0.143869
prog5	0.472444	0.162129	0.313047	0.341816	0.538699	0.187319
prog6	0.349502	0.150309	0.246029	0.319937	0.423439	0.173382
prog7	0.474593	0.155357	0.706375	0.353391	0.429722	0.174587
prog8	0.454055	0.162108	0.489904	0.378833	0.456837	0.180764
prog9	0.352266	0.162785	0.249682	0.356974	0.379867	0.184710
prog10	0.487832	0.150246	1.147667	0.368760	0.362686	0.165526
prog11	0.150312	0.156798	−0.191312	0.348383	0.294228	0.178148
prog12	0.504675	0.162575	0.619832	0.336523	0.493344	0.190111
prog13	0.096408	0.141582	0.057808	0.328764	0.107226	0.157478
prog14	0.504616	0.231745	−0.077204	0.488971	0.704036	0.272176
prog15	0.255889	0.173672	0.340903	0.304249	0.431983	0.259213
prog16	0.565426	0.141891	0.832228	0.341256	0.501983	0.156877
prog17	0.821228	0.191524	1.059671	0.345571	0.835560	0.249206
prog18	0.555256	0.163711	0.289337	0.334214	0.779683	0.196836
prog19	0.836784	0.150377	0.814994	0.317851	0.854223	0.173647

	All 2000 applicants		Award in 2000		Rejected in 2000	
	Coef.	Std. Err.	Coef.	Std. Err.	Coef.	Std. Err.
prog20	0.244477	0.141854	−0.237146	0.329318	0.404075	0.159868
prog22	0.195651	0.161614	0.228354	0.316007	0.207724	0.197363
prog24	0.414045	0.165028	0.701392	0.353119	0.361241	0.188559
prog25	0.321913	0.165101	0.430980	0.337196	0.333488	0.194467
prog26	0.102475	0.507262			0.788664	0.631251
prog28	−0.130583	0.178377	−0.342529	0.374012	−0.017864	0.206081
prog29	0.296007	0.158968	0.100322	0.320715	0.530792	0.192771
prog30	0.484486	0.145138	0.670936	0.317054	0.453005	0.165039
prog31	0.188473	0.140576	0.284433	0.355071	0.154871	0.154075
Constant	−0.568214	0.114912	−0.706182	0.265259	−0.526470	0.128456
Observations	3,598		974		2,621	
Log likelihood	−2379.6639		−612.06689		−1722.2883	

	All 2000 applicants		Award in 2000		Rejected in 2000	
	Coef.	Std. Err.	Coef.	Std. Err.	Coef.	Std. Err.

Regression Coefficients and Standard Errors for NSOPF and SDR

	Whether funded		Amount of funding	
	Coef.	Std. Err.	Coef.	Std. Err.
SDR				
Female	−0.006790	0.032136		
Experience	0.032897	0.005965		
Experience sq	−0.000950	0.000150		
Tenure-track	−0.364670	0.033351		
Computer science & math				
Life sciences	0.674314	0.047604		
Physical sciences	0.569242	0.052545		
Social sciences	−0.268270	0.049381		
Engineers	0.682936	0.057433		
Constant	−0.206590	0.061954		
Observations	8,645			
Log likelihood	−5398.2742			
NSOPF				
Female	0.030343	0.064849	0.023334	0.089611
Tenured	0.014995	0.087548	0.078006	0.114897
Tenure track	0.006737	0.083957	−0.048618	0.119068
Professional degree	−0.334866	0.092122	0.101159	0.129760
Experience	−0.023329	0.004051	0.003494	0.005510
Peer-reviewed publications	0.458070	0.032087	0.202805	0.045438
Non-peer-reviewed publications	−0.001022	0.001257	0.001845	0.001612
Texts & monographs	0.007939	0.003607	−0.001956	0.003806
Patents, software	−0.003973	0.013794	0.041238	0.016585
Natural sciences				
Social sciences & history	−0.909065	0.112398	−0.741431	0.177012
Psychology	−0.638386	0.133762	−0.117095	0.187011
Physical science	−0.015172	0.113261	−0.249997	0.120403
Math & statistics	−0.453278	0.137061	−0.670528	0.179129
Health sciences	−0.484383	0.092058	−0.031490	0.116338
Engineering	−0.158442	0.112905	−0.025443	0.129064
Education	−1.122698	0.143199	0.156709	0.235114
Computer science	−0.265010	0.167287	0.130092	0.220359
Agriculture	−0.350646	0.165470	−0.513756	0.198049
Other field	−1.525544	0.241787	0.193769	0.367145
Constant	−0.801313	0.127418	11.670050	0.184355
Observations	2,591		929	
Log likelihood	−1398.8725		−12443.0311	

E. Academic Interviews

To supplement our understanding of the role of federal grants in research organizations, we conducted informal telephone interviews with ten informants knowledgeable about research at the kinds of institutions where researchers who apply for federal grants are employed. They included deans, vice presidents, and department chairs with responsibility for research at public and private universities in fields such as agriculture, physics, economics, mathematics, and medicine. Questions concerned:

- The importance and role of grant funding for the institution,

- Expectations about how much federal grant funding should be obtained and at what point in careers,

- The existence of "soft money" positions and federal grant funding expectations for staff in these positions,

- Efforts institutions make to assist faculty and staff in obtaining funding, and

- Specific assistance efforts directed at women.

Results

Most institutions reported that federal grant funds were important in terms of prestige and financial support. Obtaining federal grant support is a sign of institutional and departmental prestige that is important in attracting high-quality students and faculty and for impressing state governors and legislatures and other funders, such as foundations. Several reported they had strategic plans featuring substantial increases in federal grant funding and indicated that, since research was a critical part of the mission, funding for research was critical to carrying out the mission. Only one department chair was lukewarm about federal grant funding, pointing to problems filling teaching assignments if faculty "bought out" their time. All but one informant said that faculty in hard money positions were expected to obtain grant funding as soon as possible, with some slack allowed in the first few years, and that grant funding is a factor in tenure decisions. One informant stated, "Basic sciences are being weaned off hard money."

73

Being a principal investigator was viewed as an important indicator of career success by most informants, although several indicated that in fields where there are large collaborative groups being a PI was less important than in other fields where grants tended to be more individual. Several mentioned a dilemma — while being a PI was a valued indicator of individual success, it conflicted with the goal of developing collaborative research. One informant said that being a co-investigator would count for promotion only if there was a demonstration of independent effort as part of the grant.

The size of grants was less frequently viewed as important than being the recipient of a grant. Several mentioned that it was valuable in terms of obtaining laboratory or office space for research activities and that institutions valued indirect funds, but most informants said that research productivity was as important as the dollar value of grants.

All but two of our informants reported the existence of "soft money" positions that are funded entirely from grants and contracts. In most cases, these were viewed as less prestigious positions and typically do not lead to obtaining tenure. In medical institutions, the soft money positions were common and, while hard money positions were still viewed as more prestigious, the staff in soft money positions were treated as equals and worked as part of collaborative teams. Some of these positions are continued only for the duration of a specific project; others are more permanent. Federal grant funds are very important for sustaining soft money positions. Most informants reported that staff in soft money positions unless the necessary funding was in place and individuals in these positions were expected to keep themselves funded or leave.

Most informants reported that the competition for federal grant funds was getting stiffer. While a few said funding in their area was increasing or perceived that it was increasing in other areas, most expected a stagnation or decline in availability of funding in their fields. They reported more effort to obtain funding, including resubmissions of grants. Despite this, most reported little organized effort to assist faculty in obtaining funding. Most reported the existence of institutional budgeting support and some formal and informal mentoring within departments, but a few reported specific programs to assist grant writers, including paying former study section members to act as internal reviewers, editorial help, formal courses on "grantsmanship," and deans holding tailored discussions with individual faculty members.

No one reported that his or her institution tracks applications or awards for grant funding or has programs that specifically assist women faculty or staff in obtaining federal grant funding. However, one informant was eloquent on the subject of the special issues that women face in balancing work and family in highly competitive scientific fields, stating that even fairly brief (three-month) breaks in career progression could be critical in terms of grants and publications with effects that would last for years, if not for the life of a career.

References

Barzansky, B., and S. I. Etzel, "Educational Programs in U.S. Medical Schools," *JAMA,* Vol. 290, No. 9, 2003, pp. 1190–1196.

Benjamin, E., "Disparities in the Salaries and Appointments of Academic Women and Men: An Update of a 1998 Report of Committee W on the Status of Women in the Academic Profession," *Academe,* Vol. 1, 1999, pp. 60–62.

Beyer, J. M., R. G. Chanove, and W. B. Fox, "The Review Process and the Fates of Manuscripts Submitted to AMJ," *Academy of Management Journal,* Vol. 38, No. 5, 1995, pp. 1219–1260.

Blake, M., and I. La Valle, *Who Applies for Research Funding? Key Factors Shaping Funding Application Behaviour Among Women and Men in British Higher Education Institutions,* London: National Centre for Social Research, 2000.

Blank, R. M., "The Effects of Double-Blind Versus Single-Blind Reviewing: Experimental Evidence from the *American Economic Review,*" *American Economic Review,* Vol. 81, No. 5, 1991, pp. 1041–1067.

Broder, I., "Review of NSF Economic Proposals: Gender and Institutional Patterns," *American Economic Review,* Vol. 83, No. 4, 1993, pp. 964–970.

Buntin, M., and A. Zaslavsky, "Too Much Ado About Two-Part Models and Transformation? Comparing Methods of Modeling Health Care Costs," *Journal of Health Economics,* Vol. 23, No. 3, 2004, pp. 525–542.

Cole, J. R., and S. Cole, "Which Researcher Will Get the Grant?" *Nature,* Vol. 279, June 14, 1979, pp. 575–576.

Duan, N., "Smearing Estimate: A Nonparametric Retransformation Method," *Journal of the American Statistical Association,* Vol. 78, No. 383, 1983, pp. 605–610.

Gillespie, G. W., Jr., D. E. Chubin, and G. Kurzon, "Experience with NIH Peer Review: Researchers' Cynicism and Desire for Change," *Science, Technology, and Human Values,* Vol. 10, No. 3, 1985, pp. 44–54.

Grant, J., S. Burden, et al., "No Evidence of Sexism in Peer Review," *Nature,* Vol. 390, 1997, p. 438.

Grant, J., and L. Low, *Women and Peer Review: An Audit of the Wellcome Trust's Decision Making on Grants,* London: Wellcome Trust, 1997.

Grant, L., and K. B. Ward, "Gender and Publishing in Sociology," *Gender and Society,* Vol. 5, No. 2, 1991, pp. 207–223.

Liao, T. F., *Interpreting Probability Models: Logit, Probit, and Other Generalized Linear Models,* Newbury Park, Calif.: Sage Publications, 1994.

Lombardi, J. V., E. D. Capaldi, et al., *The Top American Research Universities,* Tallahassee, Fla.: *TheCenter* at the University of Florida, 2003.

Long, J. S., ed., *From Scarcity to Visibility: Gender Differences in the Careers of Doctoral Scientists and Engineers,* Washington, D.C.: National Academy Press, 2001.

Manning, W., A. Basu, and J. Mullahy, "Generalized Modeling Approaches to Risk Adjustment of Skewed Outcomes Data," National Bureau of Economic Research, Technical Working Paper 293, 2003.

Mastriani, M. and S. Plattner, "Cultural Anthropology Research Support at the National Science Foundation, 1991–95," *Human Organization,* Vol. 56, 1997, pp. 121-125.

National Science Foundation (NSF), *Gender Differences in the Careers of Academic Scientists and Engineers: A Literature Review,* Project Officer, Alan Rapoport, NSF 03-322, 2003.

_____, *Gender Differences in the Careers of Academic Scientists and Engineers,* Project Officer, Alan Rapoport, NSF 04-323, 2004.

Rong, X. L., L. Grant, and K. B. Ward, "Productivity of Women Scholars and Gender Researchers: Is Funding a Factor? *American Sociologist,* Vol. 20, 1989, pp. 95–100.

Sigelman, L., and F. P. Scioli, Jr., "Retreading Familiar Terrain: Bias, Peer Review, and the NSF Political Science Program," *Political Science,* Vol. 20, No. 1, 1987, pp. 62–69.

Thornton, S., "Extended Tenure Clock Policies: Theory . . . and Practice," *CSWEP Newsletter,* 2005, pp. 13–15.

Travis, G. D. L., and H. M. Collins, "New Light on Old Boys: Cognitive and Institutional Particularism in the Peer Review System," *Science, Technology, and Human Values,* Vol. 16, No. 3, 1991, pp. 322–341.

Unger, R. K., "Through the Looking Glass: No Wonderland Yet! The Reciprocal Relationship Between Methodology and Models of Reality," *Psychology of Women Quarterly,* Vol. 8, 1983, pp. 9–32.

Watkins, S. C., "If All We Knew About Woman Was What We Read in *Demography,* What Would We Know?" *Demography,* Vol. 30, No. 4, 1993, pp. 551–577.

Wennerås, C., and A. Wold, "Nepotism and Sexism in Peer Review," *Nature,* Vol. 387, May 22, 1997, pp. 341–343.